THE
LONG
DISPATCHES ON ALASKA HISTORY
VIEW

ROSS COEN

The Long View: Dispatches on Alaska History
Cataloging-in-Publication
© 2011 by Ross Coen. All rights reserved.

Published in Ester, Alaska
by the Ester Republic Press
P.O. Box 24, Ester, AK 99725, U.S.A.
www.esterrepublic.com • info@esterrepublic.com

Printed in the United States of America
by Thomson-Shore, Inc.

Design and layout by
5th Avenue Design & Graphics, Inc.

Edited by Deirdre Helfferich

Columns reprinted in chapters 41 and 42 first
published in the *Anchorage Daily News*.
All others first published in *The Ester Republic*.

Cover photo of abandoned car in Anvik, Alaska
taken by the author in October 2009.

ISBN: 978-0-9749221-7-1 (paperback)
Library of Congress Control Number: 2011945099

ESTER REPUBLIC PRESS
PO Box 24, Ester AK 99725
www.esterrepublic.com

TABLE *of* CONTENTS

Table of Contents

FOREWORD
by Mike Hawfield

MANY OUTSTANDING HISTORIES of Alaska give the broad picture of the state's rich past, and numerous excellent and entertaining books offer various topics from fishing to homesteading to mining and much more. But there is usually little room in these books for the precious insights to people and culture, with all the ironies, surprises, and contradictions that lie at the heart of most of the stories we all enjoy telling about ourselves, our neighbors, our leaders, and the great events that have shaped Alaska.

Ross Coen's well-informed, always delightful, and sometimes surprising columns, "The Long View: Dispatches on Alaska History," expose readers to much of what is so special about Alaska and especially the true heart of Alaska: its small communities. The columns gathered here appeared over the past four years in *The Ester Republic*, a wonderfully eccentric journal published in the eccentric small town of Ester near Fairbanks. In this collection Coen gives readers more than forty great stories about our place and its people. Among these are some familiar topics, such as the careers of popular Senator Bob Bartlett, the wild election of James Wickersham in 1908, or the place of oil in Alaska's recent growth, but most stories are less familiar. Readers will be delighted to find out about the extraordinary fires at the Cleary Summit Ski Lodge and the amazing 1880s expedition of Henry Allen (a journey to rival Lewis and Clark), or the heartbreaking efforts of Austrian national Reinhard Neuhauser (a UAA graduate and skiing great) to take a job back in Alaska in the face of immigration nightmares. I suspect that many readers will identify with the tale of driving up the ALCAN and all the crazy things that can happen on that notorious highway. He also tells the amazing story of the strange "screaming fires across the Alaska skies" in 2008, and the always engaging tale of Joe Vogler's contrarian career on the Alaska stage. Other "dispatches" explore "the myth of Alaska exceptionalism," the explosive issues surrounding snow machine access to Denali National Park, Alaskans' intense aversion to taxes, their love affair with the Permanent Fund, and much more.

Some readers may see in Coen's columns an echo of the spirit of Stephen Haycox's well-known columns that have appeared over many years in the *Anchorage Daily News*. But there is something very new here. Coen gives us a fresh view garnered from the community of Ester and from the spirit of *The Ester Republic*. One of the characteristics of Coen's work I like the best is the way he presents a topic of familiarity, such as the statue of University of Alaska president Charles Bunnell on the Fairbanks campus—most students recognize it but don't know a thing about it. Like so many statues, or parks, highways, glaciers, lakes, and mountains, most of today's Alaskans know the place or the monument but have very little sense of why these everyday parts of our world are named as they are. Coen gives us the statue and the other places, and gives us a good story, but then, wonderfully, he takes us beyond this by making connections, expanding the story to other, similar or related places and events in the Alaska heritage. And, best of all, he puts all this into larger contexts, whether global, national, or state or simply back to our communities and ourselves.

Anyone who has traveled the state and has had the privilege of spending even a little time in its small communities quickly finds that each has its own unique character, its own unique way of viewing the larger world around it, and—perhaps most important—its own good sense of humor. Free-thinking Alaskans love to expose the foibles of the grandees and the powerful, or reveal the hypocrisies of pretentious behavior and the outrages of crooked characters, but we also take heart at the selfless deeds and actions of so many of our fellow travelers in Alaska communities. Every Alaska bar, café, dockside, and coffee shop is full of pundits. Readers of Coen's collection of his "The Long View" columns will either recognize themselves in the conversation or will be able to recall a friend, neighbor, or companion commenting on the great Alaskan story.

These stories are short, lively and highly readable. They are always enjoyable and they are always well-informed. Coen's stories are guaranteed to keep the reader turning pages with a smile, looking forward to the next fascinating story. The only disappointment was turning the page on the final "long view" in the collection and realizing there were no more— for now.

PREFACE

The chapters of this book were first published over a four-year period in *The Ester Republic*, a quirky periodical printed in a quirkier town of the same name. A few words of explanation are required.

Ester, Alaska is a town of roughly 2,000 people where poets, artists, and ex-hippies not only rub elbows with miners, firefighters, and bulldozer operators—sometimes the same person is all of those things. They are free-thinkers one and all, irreverent folk who enjoy each other and living in Ester immensely, often to the bafflement of those who live elsewhere and consequently fail to grasp the appeal of, for example, a fashion show of homemade aprons. Yes, they did that. The Ester Fourth of July Parade, to cite another example, features on any given year a troupe of local women playing ukuleles, a congressional candidate riding a recumbent bicycle, ballerinas in pink tutus pirouetting down the street, local farmers handing out carrots, radishes, and pea pods to the crowd, and enough political satire to prove that the town's biting wit knows no party affiliation. (When Sarah Palin resigned the Alaska governorship on July 3, 2009, that left more than enough time for Esterites to fill the next day's parade with zingers.)

Just about seven miles outside of Fairbanks is the easiest way to describe its location, though Esterites would say that Fairbanks is about seven miles outside of Ester. They exist in relation to no one. The story of how Ester became its own "Republic" is best told by lifelong resident Deirdre Helfferich:

> *Once upon a time (1986, I think), Joe Ryan, then-member of the Fairbanks North Star Borough Assembly, proposed that land in the borough, lots of it, be rezoned. In particular, he wanted the entirety of Ester Dome rezoned as mining-only land—including downtown Ester. Esterites turned out in*

> *force at the assembly hearings on the matter, telling Mr. Ryan*
> *where he could put his idea. Ryan got annoyed and accused*
> *those good citizens of living in "the People's Republic of Ester."*
> *The proposal failed, and, unfortunately for him, a lot of said*
> *Esterites were capitalists with a perverse sense of humor and*
> *took to referring to their village by Ryan's epithet. It stuck.*

Deirdre later launched a community periodical which she christened *The Ester Republic*. In its first decade of publication as the Republic's "national rag," it has served as the linguistic outlet for the locals' unique brand of irreverence. It features recipes. Its writers and cartoonists sometimes win awards.

The series of events that led to the book you are now holding in your hands began with an obscure, third-party candidate for governor who, in 2006, advocated the use of blimps to transport Alaska North Slope natural gas to market. As a historian who has studied oil and gas transportation systems in the Arctic, I knew this wild idea had been proposed (and dismissed) before. I penned a column on the cyclical nature of industrial development schemes in Alaska's oil industry (reprinted here as Chapter 1) where no idea is too ridiculous to consider again and again. Another column on Alaska boosterism followed (Chapter 2), which got me thinking of the many ways Alaska history is like a late-night movie that is re-aired every now and then on the public access channel. You know exactly what's going to happen, but you watch anyway. History doesn't actually repeat itself—except when it sort of does. I pitched Deirdre on the idea of a regular column on Alaska history. *Where we've been is a pretty good indicator of where we are now and a road map to where we're going.* She agreed.

While casting about for an appropriate column heading, one that would infer its historical focus, I first considered La Longue Durée, a phrase used by French historians to suggest that understanding any particular event or issue requires consideration of the larger historical context under which it occurred. That seemed right, but I opted for the English translation: The Long View.

The first column appeared in November 2006 and has run more or less monthly since. Often I take an item from the current Alaska news cycle and describe its historical antecedents, as is the case in Chapter 6, where oil executive Bill Allen's bribery of certain legislators brought to mind other political scandals of years past. Sometimes a historical anniversary occasions a column of remembrance, as in Chapter 18 on the centennial of James Wickersham's election to Congress. And still other columns result from no particular cause, but are only good stories worth telling.

The topic of each column, I must note, is only half the point. History is more than just names, places, and dates; it's an attempt to understand a particular era and the circumstances that made the events of that time possible. What was happening in Alaska in March 1959, for example, that made the arrival of some homesteaders from Michigan such a big deal (see Chapter 22)? How was the lopsided male-to-female ratio in Fairbanks in 1908 a function of the gold rush economy (see Chapter 10)? What can the anti-statehood arguments of the 1940s and 50s tell us about the economic condition of Alaska at that time (see Chapter 15)? It is these types of larger questions I attempt to answer (or at least address) in each column. Every historical event occurs within a particular context unique to that place and time. And that, I believe, is something worth knowing.

A few words about the book's format the reader should find helpful: This book contains four years' worth of columns, printed here in the order in which they were first published in *The Ester Republic*, along with two additional columns from the *Anchorage Daily News*. In cases where columns were first published as a two- or three-part series across multiple editions, they have been compressed here into a single chapter. A handful of columns were pegged to particular historical anniversaries that occurred at the time of publication—a topical device that means nothing in this collected volume—thus references to "one hundred years ago this month," for instance, have been either clarified or removed.

I have placed at the start of each chapter a brief paragraph introducing the topic. This might include an explanation of how or why the column was written, or additional information not included in the original version. The reader will also note this volume is not, nor claims to be, a comprehensive overview of Alaska history. The topics are all over the map and were chosen with the intent of telling a good story *about* Alaska, not the entire story *of* Alaska.

One final note: Readers of this book will quickly discern that its chapters are not the dispassionate works of a neutral observer. Although historians are not supposed to take sides, the outspoken nature of the publication in which these columns first appeared seemed to invite statements of commentary. It was an invitation I found easy to accept. Any differences of opinion between the reader and the author would best be explored in full public view with clever, slightly barbed letters to the editor in *The Ester Republic*, P.O. Box 24, Ester, AK 99725. Points will be given, according to Deirdre, for well-written prose displaying good taste, irreverent and witty humor, things said that need to be said, and good, useful, constructive criticism.

Ross Coen
August 5, 2011

BOASTING
HOT AIR AGAIN
or
FLOATING
SOME OLD IDEAS

✦✦✦✦✦

The roster of proposed (but never realized) development schemes in Alaska reads like a science fiction writer's notebook of story ideas—a tunnel under the Bering Strait connecting Alaska and Russia, a freshwater pipeline to California, and a hydroelectric dam on the Yukon River that would not only generate gigawatts of power for one of the most sparsely populated regions in the country but also flood an area the size of Vermont. Big thinkers, as this column shows, have never been lacking in Alaska.

THOMAS EDISON, THE story goes, once admitted that for every great idea he came up with—and he had a lot of those—there were a thousand duds that never quite panned out. One imagines a similar ratio when it comes to industrial development schemes in Alaska. Our state is a veritable repository of far-our proposals that in a charitable mood we might call innovative.

To wit, Libertarian candidate for governor Billy Toien has advocated not a pipeline, but a fleet of airships to transport North Slope gas to market. That's right, dirigibles. Blimps. Hey, when your cargo itself is lighter than air why not fill up a giant balloon and steer it south? The Alaska booster spirit lives!

Artist's 1969 sketch of an elevated pipeline/highway combo, one of the many Prudhoe Bay crude oil transportation proposals. Note the many drilling rigs in the background and the aurora borealis in the sky overhead. ALASKA CONSTRUCTION & OIL, OCTOBER 1969, PAGE 61

What Toien likely knows, though the average Alaska may not, is that this same idea was floated (pun fully intended) in 1968 to transport crude from Prudhoe Bay. Back then there were dozens of such inventive transportation proposals, all of which fell neatly into the booster tradition of technological solutions to overcome every obstacle to development.

Proponents of the blimp idea emphasized the relatively minimal ground-based infrastructure of the system and corresponding slight environmental impact. They couldn't, however, solve the problem that two million barrels of crude oil (the estimated daily production at Prudhoe Bay) are really, really heavy.

In 1972 Boeing unveiled the design of a fixed-wing aircraft tanker with twelve jet engines, a 478-foot wingspan, and an 83-foot tail. Crude would be loaded into two wing-mounted pods, each measuring 150 feet long and 26 feet in diameter. The plane's gross take-off weight would be 1,750 tons. Did I mention crude oil is heavy?

General Dynamics came along with a proposal for nuclear submarines to ferry the oil under the polar ice cap to New York, Europe, Japan, and beyond. Preliminary designs called for 900-foot, rectangular-hulled subs of between 170,000 and 250,000 deadweight tons. Monsters that size couldn't get anywhere near Prudhoe Bay due to the shallow seabed of the Beaufort Sea, however, and an offshore terminal with fifty miles of subsea pipelines would never survive the shifting icepack. Father of the H-bomb Edward Teller helpfully suggested that nuclear blasts could dredge a channel and excavate a deep-water harbor right at the coastline.

Exxon ran an icebreaking tanker, the SS *Manhattan*, through the fabled Northwest Passage to test the logistic and economic viability of a surface marine route. The vessel sailed from Chester, Pennsylvania to Prudhoe Bay and back in 1969, successfully transiting the ice-choked straits of the North American Arctic, but in the process demonstrated the impracticality of such a system. In other words, the ship got stuck in the ice. More than once.

A rail link to the North Slope was considered, until engineers discovered that moving a single day's production at Prudhoe Bay would require sixty-three trains of a hundred cars each. Tanker trucks also received a hearing, but it was noted that such a system required sixty thousand trucks operating every day on an eight-lane, all-weather paved road connecting Deadhorse and Fairbanks. Not going to happen.

In the end, of course, the industry built an 800-mile pipeline to Valdez that has been in continuous operation since 1977. Today we're talking about another pipeline to bring to market the trillions of cubic feet of North Slope gas, yet Toien's campaign platform demonstrates that alternative schemes, no matter how unconventional, still receive consideration.

The SS *Manhattan*, an icebreaking tanker commissioned by Humble
Oil as a possible oil transportation alternative to the trans-Alaska
pipeline. MERRITT HELFFERICH

Another gubernatorial candidate, David Massie of the Green Party, has
argued against a gas pipeline in favor of cylindrical canisters that would
be loaded with gas and sent down the existing oil line—an idea that
almost seems reasonable when compared to the many others over the
years.

Boosterism in Alaska is cyclical. The politicians change, the corporations come and go, the particulars of each project are a little different—
but the same basic ideas come around and around, again and again.

BIG
DOMES

•••••

*It's easy to poke fun at the many back-of-the-cocktail-napkin
development schemes throughout Alaska's history—such as the
domed cities described in this column—but the mere fact they
are proposed by straight-faced entrepreneurs says a lot about
the Alaskan booster mentality. This spirit is epitomized by the
biggest dreamer of them all, Governor Walter J. Hickel: "We'll
never run out of resources. The only thing we might run out of
is imagination."*

WHAT IS IT with northern people and domes? In the 1950s the
Canadian government announced plans to build a domed city called
Frobisher Bay on the inlet of the same name on Baffin Island. Here in
Alaska, you may remember, there have been proposals for enormous
domes and climate-controlled cities in Denali and Anchorage. Even in
my home state of North Dakota—which, if not exactly the Arctic, still
has the word "north" in its name and is a tad chilly in the wintertime—
there was guy a few decades back convinced that building a dome over
the small town of Parshall would…well, I can't remember precisely what
it would do except be really neat.

In the last chapter I described some of the outlandish transportation
proposals for Prudhoe Bay crude oil and how such ideas, because they
emphasized scientific ingenuity in the pursuit of overcoming environ-

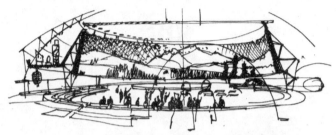

a way to bring Alaska to visitors at Denali 365 days of the year — not a substitute but a supplement

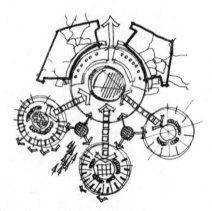

Sketches of the proposed (but never built) domed visitor's center at the Tokositna River south of Mount McKinley. The caption calls the dome "a way to bring Alaska to visitors at Denali 365 days of the year—not a substitute but a supplement." TOKOSITNA DEVELOPMENT STUDY

mental obstacles, fit squarely in the Alaska booster tradition. Now let's continue that theme with a discussion of *science as panacea*, or the idea that technological innovation can be used to solve social problems.

In the late 1970s the Alaska State Legislature formed the Tokositna Special Committee to oversee a major year-round tourism and recreation project for the Denali area. The proposal included hotels, restaurants, campgrounds, hiking trails, alpine and cross-country skiing areas, and— here comes the best part—a giant Teflon dome to enclose it all.

The presence of U.S. Senator Mike Gravel on the committee lent some gravitas to the project. The committee went so far as to commission several feasibility studies and invite participation from the private sector. The projected tourist numbers looked good and the feasibility report on skiing in Denali checked out (snow and hills being in abundant supply), but the idea never panned out. It ultimately collapsed due to several factors identified in the committee's report—the exorbitant cost, its incompatibility with the region's environment and wilderness values, and, you guessed it, unproven technologies regarding the Teflon dome.

A similar proposal had been unveiled a decade earlier for the Anchorage area. Tandy Industries, an outfit from Tulsa, Oklahoma, came to Alaska in 1969 with quite a deal for us cold-weather folk: a fully-enclosed, climate-controlled city to be built across Knik Arm from Anchorage.

The city would be named "Seward's Success" (as opposed to his "folly," get it?) and feature housing for 5,000 residents immediately with capacity for another 15,000 within a decade. The plan called for residential and commercial malls, hotels, office buildings, restaurants, churches, recreational facilities, and every other conceivable structure, all enclosed and interconnected by skyways. Cars would be prohibited, but who needs them when the moving sidewalks, escalators, and bike paths are also sealed within the superstructure. The temperature would be kept at a constant 68 degrees.

"Coats and boots will never be required," claimed Tandy's glossy, full-color brochure, "unless one traveled to Anchorage or went outside for recreation." Oh, and to get to Anchorage? A tramway across Knik Arm, naturally.

If these proposals sound almost too preposterous to be true, remember that both came along at times when the state was flush with money. Legislators dreamed up the Denali dome just as the pipeline went into operation and began delivering crude to Valdez and cash to Juneau. The press conference where Seward's Success was unveiled occurred the very same week of the 1969 Prudhoe Bay lease sale where the state took in $900 million, a figure that eclipsed the entire state budget that year by a factor of six. To a population then deprived of so many state services we take for granted today, the respective windfalls represented a chance to make life in Alaska much more comfortable. Teflon domes and climate-controlled cities certainly fit that bill.

Alfred R. Tandy, left, of Tandy Industries and architect Richard Dimit with an artist's sketch of Seward's Success, the fully enclosed, climate-controlled city Tandy proposed to build across Knik Arm from Anchorage in 1969. ANCHORAGE DAILY NEWS/MCT/LANDOV

The fundamental concept behind these proposals, and countless others in Alaska for that matter, is that the application of science and technology can subdue the natural environment, make people's lives easier, and thus be used a tool to cure all manner of social ills. The promoters of Seward's Success said as much when they explicitly compared the easy living of their northern utopia to the pollution, congestion, and general social strife of cities in the Lower 48. (Unemployment, economic hardship, health problems, environmental degradation? Not in my climate-controlled dome!)

Call it the Alaska version of technological determinism—the belief that scientific innovation is always on the forward march. As the driving force behind societal change, technology and invention are the keys to prosperity and the solution to social problems. Think back to the heroes of your grade school history textbook: Eli Whitney, Thomas Edison,

Alexander Graham Bell, Henry Ford. We celebrate inventors not so much for their creations themselves, but for the changes they produced in society, the ways they made our lives better, and the America they built.

It's largely because we live in the North, where the obstacles to development posed by the natural world so often require technological solutions on a grand scale, that we are so fascinated by every application of that technology. That so many wild schemes never materialize, including those described above, is less important than what they tell us about our character and collective views regarding our relationship with science.

Yet finding solutions to social problems often requires value judgments, too. Science can be an incredible tool for identifying and even mitigating such problems, but it is up to the user of that science to consider ethics and morals in the application. Science itself may have no intrinsic values, but there is no such thing as value-free science. Just because we can build a dome—or a dam, or a pipeline, or whatever—doesn't necessarily mean we should.

MINORITY
LAWMAKERS
PAST
and
PRESENT

♦♦♦♦♦

On January 3, 1984, the silver anniversary of Alaska state-hood, sixty-eight men and women named "Founders of Alaska" received commemorative medals at a gala celebration in Fairbanks. Among the honorees were former governors, leg-islators, mayors, educators, and all-around sourdoughs. One dignitary too ill to attend was Frank Peratrovich who, as this column points out, had a long and distinguished public career. Peratrovich's name was called out to great applause and his medal presented in absentia. He died the following day.

WHEN THE 25TH Alaska State Legislature convened in January 2007, there was a single Asian-American, Scott Kawasaki of Fairbanks, among the lawmakers taking the oath. The first-term Democrat followed a trail blazed by Thelma Buchholdt of Anchorage. Elected to the State House in 1974, she was the first Asian-American legislator in Alaska and the first Filipino woman to serve in a legislative body in the entire U.S. Buch-holdt served four terms in the House and later was the driving force behind the Asian Alaskan Cultural Center.

Another minority lawmaker serving with Kawasaki in 2007 was Senator Bettye Davis, the only African-American in the sixty-member legislature. Her pioneering predecessor was Blanche L. McSmith, like Davis a Democrat from Anchorage. McSmith became the first African-

11

Delegates to the Alaska Constitutional Convention held at the University of Alaska, 1955-1956. HISTORICAL PHOTOGRAPH COLLECTION, UAF-1966-9-28, ALASKA AND POLAR REGIONS, RASMUSON LIBRARY, UNIVERSITY OF ALASKA FAIRBANKS

American legislator when Governor Bill Egan appointed her in January 1960 to fill a seat vacated by John Rader, who had left the House to become attorney general.

The nine Alaska Natives in the 2007 legislature followed in the footsteps of William Paul who was elected to the territorial legislature in 1924. In addition to being the first Alaska Native to hold such a position, Paul was the first to become an attorney and, along with his brother Louis, turned the Alaska Native Brotherhood into a political force.

In the roster of trailblazing minorities, however, perhaps the most notable is a merchant and fisherman from Klawock named Frank Peratrovich who served as a delegate to the Alaska Constitutional Convention in 1955–56.

There is a photograph, I'm sure you've seen it, of the fifty-five Alaskans who met that winter on the university campus in Fairbanks to write the founding document for the future state. The delegates are arranged in four rows, the first seated on the floor. Your eye is drawn to the center of the photograph where Bill Egan, the convention's president and the man

Frank Peratrovich
CONSTITUTIONAL
CONVENTION DELEGATE
PHOTOGRAPHS, UAF-1983-
185-18, ALASKA AND POLAR
REGIONS, RASMUSON
LIBRARY, UNIVERSITY OF
ALASKA FAIRBANKS

who would become the state's first governor, is seated. Perhaps it's the filter of history tinged with nostalgia for a better time when we Alaskans thought of ourselves as one, but you see in the photo a tenacity of purpose in those pioneers. No one thinks of the heated arguments that most certainly took place, or even the personal conflicts that any group of this size would be forced to endure. We remember them as venerable pioneers who authored a magnificent constitution.

But you notice something else in the photo, too. It occurs to you slowly, gradually, until it's that one thing you cannot help but notice every subsequent time you look at it. There are a lot of white men. A lot. There are a few women, also white, scattered here and there. If you're looking for minorities among the delegates, say an Alaska Native, well there's Peratrovich in the second row. He's the only one—in a territory where Alaska Natives comprised roughly 18 per cent of the total population at the time.

This is not a criticism of the group. Never before or since has such an august group of Alaskans gathered to work so selflessly toward our collective best interests. We owe them enormous gratitude. Yet there is no denying that the assembly of delegates looks very much like a banker's convention in Topeka.

It would be a mistake, however, to suggest that Peratrovich was something of a token representative on the body. The events of the convention's second day, November 9, 1955, proved otherwise. Egan, having already been installed as the convention president, called for the election of the First Vice President. George Sundborg of Juneau rose to put forth a nomination:

His ancestors have been born in Alaska as far back over as many generations as this land was populated by human beings. He, too, has been a member of the Territorial Legislature serving with distinction in both the House and the Senate, and he…has been the President of the Senate of the Alaska Territorial Legislature. I would particularly like to see this Convention honor the nominee who I am about to name, by giving him a position of high rank in the Convention, because he is a member of the aboriginal inhabitants of this Territory, a representative of the Indian people who lived here long before any of the rest of us came on the scene. And the man whose nomination I now urge upon you is Frank Peratrovich of Klawock.

Three other delegates received nominations for the post: James Nolan, Mildred Hermann, and Michael Walsh. As the ballots were being distributed, Seaborn Buckalew, Jr., indecorously called out, "How do you spell Peratrovich?" Buckalew's choice earned the most votes, 18, but did not receive a clear majority. A second ballot followed with similar results, leading to the two lowest vote getters, Hermann and Walsh, being dropped from consideration.

In the third ballot for First Vice President, Peratrovich received 28 votes to Nolan's 26.

Only a decade earlier, signs reading "No Natives Allowed" were posted in restaurants, hotels, and other public places throughout Alaska. Now an Alaska Native was the second chair of the convention writing the state constitution.

Peratrovich himself was absent the day he was elected to the post. Heavy clouds in Klawock had kept his plane on the ground for several days. Not until the fifth day of the convention did he walk into the hall in Fairbanks to a round of applause from his fellow delegates.

GUBERNATORIAL
OPERATIONS

Of all the clauses in the Alaska State Constitution, no one would have guessed that the first to be invoked on the first day of statehood would be the one providing for the transfer of executive power from the governor to his deputy. Yet that's just what happened on January 3, 1959, when Governor Bill Egan fell ill just hours after taking the oath of office. This two-part series explores two different cases of gubernatorial incapacitation—Egan's and that of Frank Murkowski four decades later—and the dissimilar handling of each.

I. A TEMPORARY ABSENCE FROM OFFICE

Gubernatorial inaugurations are always festive affairs. The air crackles with the promise of a fresh start. The state's very first inauguration was one like no other.

On the morning of January 3, 1959, Bill Egan was awaiting a phone call from Washington, DC. Egan had been elected the state's first governor the previous November. Joining him by the telephone that morning in Juneau were Hugh Wade, the secretary of state-elect (a position we now call lieutenant governor), the families of both men, a few members of the governor-elect's staff, and two representatives from the post office on hand to officially postmark the first day covers. Judge Raymond F. Kelly stood by holding a Bible that had been presented to Egan by the First Baptist Church in Juneau.

A gaunt Bill Egan takes the oath of office on January 3, 1959. Later that
day he would be rushed to the hospital for emergency gall bladder surgery.
WILLIAM A. EGAN COLLECTION, 87-055-02N, BOX 108, FOLDER 7, ALASKA AND
POLAR REGIONS, RASMUSON LIBRARY, UNIVERSITY OF ALASKA FAIRBANKS

Shortly after 9:00 a.m., the phone rang with news that President
Dwight Eisenhower had just signed the official proclamation admitting
Alaska as the 49th state. Kelly immediately administered the oath of office
to Egan and the State of Alaska had its first governor. (The oath, inciden-
tally, required Egan to swear that he was not a member of the Communist
Party or any other subversive group that advocated the overthrow of the
United States government.)

Two hours later, Egan delivered his inaugural address before a crowd
of eight hundred jubilant Alaskans at a downtown theatre. Two hours
after that, Egan was in the hospital being prepped for major surgery.

During a four-hour operation at St. Ann's Hospital, doctors removed
Egan's gall bladder, as well as a stone from the common bile duct. His

condition was reported as good, though the lead physician informed reporters that the governor would be "unable to transact any business for a few days." That would prove to be an astounding understatement.

Egan soon developed a life-threatening case of acute pancreatitis, a not uncommon condition following gall bladder surgery, and had to be flown to a hospital in Seattle. He remained there throughout the spring of 1959, undergoing several additional surgeries to control the pancreatic inflammation and remove an intestinal blockage. Not until the closing days of the legislative session in April did Egan regain his health and return to Juneau to formally assume his duties as governor.

Fortunately for Alaskans, the state constitution provided for such an unusual occurrence. Article 3, Section 9 states: "In case of the temporary absence of the governor from office, the lieutenant governor shall serve as acting governor."

Hugh Wade thus found himself serving as Alaska's chief executive on the first day of statehood. As Wade himself later admitted, he wasn't altogether certain he was up to the task. Egan was a notorious workaholic who had taken charge of quite literally every task all on his own. He had barely given Wade an hour of his time in the months leading up to statehood. But by surrounding himself with competent officials held over from the territorial government, Wade executed the office capably throughout the spring and today receives favorable marks from historians for his performance.

Like so many other constitutional provisions this one appears both patently clear and frustratingly vague. Exactly what is meant by a governor's "temporary absence...from office" seems a question left to the judgment of the attorney general. The case of Bill Egan, falling gravely ill just hours after being sworn in, clearly qualifies.

Yet you may remember a more recent case involving the hospitalization of a governor where it appears no one consulted the constitution. I refer to Frank Murkowski's angioplasty operation in April 2003, which only a select group of people even knew about until after the fact.

II. THE HEART OF LAWS AND MEN

"In case of the temporary absence of the governor from office, the lieuten-ant governor shall serve as acting governor." So reads Article 3, Section 9 of the Alaska State Constitution on matters of gubernatorial succession. Forty-four years after that clause was exercised during Bill Egan's hospi-talization, another governor was rushed to the hospital with what his doctors deemed a very serious condition. In that case, Article 3, Section 9 was not invoked. In fact, it appears not even to have been considered.

On the afternoon of Wednesday, April 9, 2003, Governor Frank Murkowski wasn't feeling well. He had been traveling that week and arrived back home in Juneau complaining of fatigue and dehydration. Following a quick trip to the local hospital, Jim Clark, the governor's chief of staff, announced to reporters that Murkowski, in an apparent abundance of caution, was being flown to Providence Medical Center in Anchorage for what he called "routine tests."

In point of fact, the doctors in Juneau suspected a serious problem with the governor's heart. Murkowski underwent a procedure to open a branch of the left coronary artery, which doctors discovered was 95 to 98 percent blocked. The 20-minute procedure went off without a hitch and within hours Murkowski was munching on a sandwich, complaining about the uncomfortable hospital bed, and asking when he could go home.

From a constitutional perspective there are a number of serious problems with the carefree manner of the governor's office.

On that Wednesday evening, there were exactly two people in all of state government who knew the true severity of the governor's condition: Murkowski himself and Jim Clark. John Manly, the governor's press secretary, admitted as much when he later told reporters that everyone else on the governor's staff, himself included, learned about the surgery only after it had been performed.

Lieutenant Governor Loren Leman? Attorney General Gregg Renkes? Senate President Gene Therriault? House Speaker Pete Kott? All remained unaware of these events as they were happening.

So keeping in mind the constitutional provision for replacing a governor who is "temporarily absen(t)...from office," one must consider a scenario where Murkowski's heart surgery had not gone as smoothly. While the procedure in question is fairly routine, any occasion for doctors to poke around in the heart of an overweight, 70-year old man with high cholesterol is cause for concern. Suppose for a moment that Murkowski had gone into cardiac arrest on the operating table or even slipped into a coma. Or worse.

Because no one apart from Frank Murkowski and Jim Clark knew precisely what was going on, the state would have been without a chief executive for as long as it took Clark to track down the attorney general and obtain a written legal opinion, find the lieutenant governor and a judge to administer the oath, and complete whatever other legal and administrative tasks would be necessary to formally transfer the duties of the office. Such an interval, of any duration, carries serious legal and practical consequences.

In the closing days of Murkowski's administration in 2006, when his approval rating was lower than that of every other governor except Ohio's (who was then under indictment on ethics charges), the governor was asked to name a few mistakes that might account for his unpopularity. He granted that his administration didn't always communicate effectively with the public.

The hubris of that sentiment notwithstanding—that Alaskans would have liked him more had he just done a better job of explaining his exceptional performance—it actually reveals something quite telling about Murkowski. In his four years as governor, not to mention the twenty-two he spent in the U.S. Senate before that, Murkowski earned a reputation for non-consultative decision-making and a ham-handed communication style. The consequences of this approach usually remained in the politi-

21

cal sphere, though Murkowski's clumsy handling of the above mentioned episode reveals an indifference to the authority of the state constitution and to the people themselves, who are not only the beneficiaries of that document but the true holders of it as well.

Future administrations, particularly those run by men with heart trouble, would be wise to remember the oft-stated dictum that we are a state of laws, not men.

on the
INCLUSION
or
EXCLUSION
of
RIGHTS

♦♦♦♦♦

The non-binding advisory vote is like a politician's escape hatch—a way to conduct the most comprehensive opinion poll possible while simultaneously avoiding having to take a stand on a controversial issue. The 2007 Alaska Advisory Vote on Same-Sex Public Employment Benefits, to call it by its official name, was one such milquetoast maneuver.

ON APRIL 3, 2007, Alaska voters went to the polls for a non-binding advisory vote on whether a constitutional amendment prohibiting employment benefits to same-sex partners of public employees should be placed on the ballot in a future election. In other words, it was an unofficial vote on whether we should hold an official vote. Just over fifty-three percent of voters cast ballots saying, yes, let's do this election again but for real next time.

It is not surprising that the authors of our state's founding document, the fifty-five delegates to the Alaska Constitutional Convention in 1955–56, remained silent on the issue of same-sex unions. Theirs was an era where decent folks pretty well kept to themselves about unions of every kind and, besides, the delegates had much more pressing matters to discuss.

There happened a debate, however, midway through the convention that is instructive for our present-day deliberations on the economic side of state-sanctioned coupledom.

On January 5, 1956, while crafting language that became the Declaration of Rights in Article 1 of the Constitution, delegates debated the respective meanings of civil, political, and religious rights, and the extent to which including only one, or maybe two of these terms adequately covered the rights expressed by all.

Then Victor Fischer, a 31-year old city planner from Anchorage, rose to ask whether "economic rights" should be added to the mix:

> *I would like to point out that we have a very large population in Alaska of people other than the white race, and I think it is important that they be given every possible protection within this constitution, that they be guaranteed every possible equality of rights and opportunity. What this does, even if we put 'economic' in here, it would only say that they may not be denied enjoyment of an economic right because of race, color, creed or national origin. In other words, it would prohibit discrimination against these people who constitute a very large number of Alaskans.*

A debate ensued whether such economic rights were already covered by the famous "life, liberty and the pursuit of happiness" clause the delegates wisely lifted from another, much older founding document. Some individuals felt that to add economic rights would open a Pandora's Box of right-to-work claims and collective bargaining. In the end, the delegates decided by a voice vote not to explicitly enshrine economic rights in the state constitution.

At no time, however, did a single delegate give voice to the idea of *excluding* any Alaskan from this or any other right. The decision to reject Fischer's amendment rested solely on the legal ambiguity of the term "economic" and the belief that such rights, however defined, were already protected by language borrowed from Messrs. Adams, Jefferson, Franklin et al.

Vic Fischer CONSTITU-
TIONAL CONVENTION
DELEGATE PHOTOGRAPHS,
UAF-1983-185-53, ALASKA
AND POLAR REGIONS,
RASMUSON LIBRARY,
UNIVERSITY OF ALASKA
FAIRBANKS

Peruse the minutes of the convention and you will find multiple cases where delegates engaged in vigorous debate for endless hours, sometimes quibbling over the correct punctuation mark, to ensure that all Alaskans would enjoy equal rights and opportunities and that basic freedoms would be forever guaranteed.

Both the constitutional amendment prohibiting same-sex marriage (which voters approved in 1998) and this latest attempt to restrict employment benefits from same-sex partners of public employees represent a shameful blot on the tremendous efforts of those fifty-five convention delegates to secure equality for all citizens. It's the first time discrimination has been enshrined in the Alaska State Constitution.

CORRUPTION,
ALASKA-STYLE

The Baranof Hotel sits on Franklin Street in Juneau just down the hill from the State Capitol. It was in Suite 604 in spring 2007, that Bill Allen, head of the oil services company VECO, plied a handful of legislators with cash, booze, and, in the case of House Speaker Pete Kott, a bottle of Viagra, in return for their votes on a package of oil taxation bills. The VECO affair shocked Alaskans—but probably shouldn't have. Alaska and corruption go way back, as this three-part series shows.

I. VECO'S DANK HISTORY

Of all the curious aspects of the VECO bribery scandal—that some legislators sold out for so little money, or that VECO chief Bill Allen wielded his influence so boldly, in one case calling legislators on their cell phones while they were casting votes on the House floor—perhaps the least surprising fact is that it happened at all. Anyone with a sense of Alaska history knows that political chicanery is never far away. Those who have paid any attention to VECO over the years are well aware of the company's propensity for pushing the ethical envelope time after time.

In the mid-1980s, officials at VECO hatched a scheme to get around the state's campaign finance laws, which limited both corporate and individual contributions to political candidates. The company encouraged

27

its employees to contribute a hundred bucks, helpfully deducted straight from payroll, and then directed the largesse to favored candidates in the guise of small, unreported contributions. Executives who contributed more were reimbursed with "bonuses." (The ploy extended to Allen's girlfriend who, bank records show, made a $1,000 deposit in her checking account and wrote a $1,000 check to a candidate the same day. Any guesses where the thousand bucks came from?)

VECO employees who objected could opt out of the scheme, though one can imagine the fortitude necessary to exercise such an option. ("Sorry, Bill, I'd rather my money not be given to pro-development, anti-environmental ideologues. But thanks for asking.") The Alaska Public Offices Commission eventually fined VECO $28,000 for the illegal scheme.

Dispensing VECO's campaign cash to compliant public officials in those days was the job of Ed Dankworth, the company's chief lobbyist. "Big Ed" was a former state senator who left office in 1982 amid questions of his own ethical transgressions. According to grand jury testimony, Dankworth signed an agreement to purchase an unused pipeline camp from Alyeska for $900,000, which he then tried to sell to the state for use as a prison. Big Ed's asking price? Three million dollars. Dankworth then used his chairmanship of the Senate Finance Committee to insert a line into the state budget allocating the funds. He was indicted in late 1982 on criminal conflict of interest charges, but the case was dropped when his lawyer successfully argued Dankworth was protected by legislative immunity.

Dankworth's political career was finished, but when he signed on as VECO's lobbyist he wielded power and influence as never before. With five-figure contributions to politicos from both parties, Dankworth organized the leadership and majority caucuses in both the Senate and House. Bills to increase oil taxes and close loopholes that were costing the state millions consistently failed to pass. In many cases the measures were bottled up in committees chaired by VECO-supported legislators.

VECO, then as now, operated as the political bulldog for the oil industry. Although the major oil companies have consistently denied any

Ed Dankworth, the legislator and VECO lobbyist at the center of many of
Alaska's political scandals of the 1980s. ANCHORAGE DAILY NEWS/MCT/LANDOV

collusion with VECO, there is no doubting that Allen's company has been
rewarded handsomely for its efforts. At the start of the 1980s, VECO was
a small industry contractor going through Chapter 11 bankruptcy. By
the end of the decade, the company was a powerhouse with contacts at
every level of state government and oil services contracts, including the
Exxon Valdez clean-up, worth hundreds of millions of dollars.

By that time Bill Allen was more than just a very wealthy man. In
1994 he was named Alaskan of the Year.

II. THE ALASKA SYNDICATE

As the FBI continues to investigate bribes paid by VECO to certain public
officials, it's worth remembering that impropriety has a long history here
on the frontier. Alaska's vast stores of natural resources, or more precisely their immense monetary worth, have long been the foundation for
all manner of scandal, bribery, policy conflicts, and expressions of outright
greed. Because corruption is universal even shenanigans of bygone eras
will sound remarkably familiar.

In 1909, an investment and development group called the Alaska Syndicate approached Secretary of the Interior Richard Ballinger to request a bit of governmental relief. The group, backed by the powerful Guggenheim mining empire and the financier J.P. Morgan, had filed mining claims some years before on thousands of acres of coal-bearing lands in Alaska—claims potentially worth millions but whose development had to date been stymied by Interior's failure to approve the group's application.

Could Ballinger, the Syndicate wondered, speed up that process?

When word of the request reached Gifford Pinchot, head of the U.S. Forest Service, he saw it as yet another example of big business seeking to plunder public resources for private gain. A protégé of Teddy Roosevelt and one of the country's first environmental leaders, Pinchot championed the cause of conservation, the scientific management of natural resources for their sustained use and maximum public benefit.

Pinchot blasted Ballinger for what he believed was the latter's assault on the progressive environmental reforms of the previous decade. When his complaints to President William Taft accomplished nothing, Pinchot went public with scathing criticism of both Ballinger and the president. His actions helped to further widen the rift in the Republican Party between the Rooseveltian progressives and the more conservative wing inhabited by Taft.

This was the scandal that wasn't. There were no bribes or pay-offs, no shady dealings of any kind. The entire affair resulted from different political beliefs held by officials convinced they were right and their opponents were wrong. By the time a Congressional investigation largely cleared the Interior Department of any wrongdoing, Ballinger had resigned, Taft had fired Pinchot, and the Republican Party found itself embroiled in a bitter internal feud that ultimately threw the 1912 election to Democrat Woodrow Wilson.

The Ballinger-Pinchot affair shows how resource managers often ignore substantive policy disputes in favor of questioning the motives, character, and integrity of the people involved. The general public has little desire to obtain a thorough understanding of highly technical policy issues, but needs no help grasping that one side is always going to twist the facts in pursuit of some selfish agenda. Which side does the fact-twisting, of course, is all a matter of perspective.

Points we might otherwise consider largely irrelevant to sober public discourse—what company an individual works for, what percentage of an interest group's funding comes from Outside, how long someone has lived in Alaska, and so on—all seem to matter significantly when land, water, wildlife, and especially money are at stake.

And the Alaska coal claims, the issue that started the Ballinger-Pinchot affair a century ago? Never patented. Which perhaps shows that wealthy corporate interests such as the Alaska Syndicate (not to mention VECO) prefer just enough chaos within government to make it pliable, but not so much that the process bogs down altogether.

III. THAT'S HOW IT'S DONE

Perhaps the only way public outrage over the current political scandals in Alaska could be tempered is for folks to realize that previous generations of Alaskans had it much, much worse. Bribing elected officials to pass special interest legislation, as VECO is alleged to have done? Earmarks for pork barrel projects in return for campaign contributions, a trick Don Young has apparently perfected? That's nothing compared to the scam pulled by Alexander McKenzie and Arthur Noyes, the former a national leader in the Republican Party and the latter a federal judge in Alaska, who in 1900 outright stole the most valuable mining claims in Nome.

Now that's how corruption is done.

The story of the "three lucky Swedes" who found gold on the Seward Peninsula in 1898 is well known. Their discovery touched off bitter resentment among the true-blooded Americans who came along later. Believing (erroneously) that anyone not holding U.S. citizenship was prohibited from legally staking a mining claim, these latecomers felt entitled to jump claims and appropriate property—steal, in other words—from anyone with an accent and an ambiguous pedigree.

Enter Mr. McKenzie who saw an opportunity to do the same without even getting Alaska dirt under his fingernails.

McKenzie first established a dummy corporation that used bogus shares to "buy" disputed gold claims in Nome. He then used his high-level contacts in Congress to write legislation that would have voided all mining claims staked by non-citizens. McKenzie's scheme evaporated when conscientious senators stripped his pet amendment from the Alaska Code that passed into law.

But in a lawless place like Nome, McKenzie found it's just as effective to have a federal judge in your pocket.

Within four days of Arthur Noyes's arrival in Nome in the summer of 1900, the new district court judge invalidated five disputed mining claims and installed his good friend Alexander McKenzie as trustee. Rather than hold the claims pending judicial review, as was his assignment, McKenzie launched a furious effort to extract gold from the ground as quickly as possible.

By the time an appellate court in San Francisco overruled Noyes and ordered the immediate return of the claims to the plaintiffs, only eight weeks had passed on the calendar but hundreds of thousands of dollars worth of gold had been pilfered by the "trustee."

Like self-serving politicos throughout history, McKenzie and Noyes exploited public greed, mistrust, and xenophobia to promote their own agenda (in this case thievery). And, like the same well-connected, white-collar criminals of every era, they received barely a slap on the wrist. McKenzie spent just a few months behind bars before receiving a presidential pardon, while Noyes lost only his judicial post and served no jail time.

Corruption is indeed universal. Whether stealing at the point of a gun or the tip of a fountain pen, Alaska is pretty much like everywhere else. And always has been.

MARATHON
FEVER

*****

The Equinox Marathon is one I have suffered four times. The first year I had no idea what it meant to run a marathon and without much forethought (or training) I set a goal of finishing in under five hours. I clocked in at 6:24:31—and could barely walk for the next two days. The following year, having trained even less, I limped across the finish line in 6:56:43. For my third go I decided to forget about the clock and just enjoy a nice walk. It didn't work. My ankles hurt so badly by the end—7:42:48, by the way—that I asked my wife to remind me of the pain the following year when I knew I'd be tempted to sign up again. She reminded me. I ignored her. That year I crossed the line in 6:58:51 and reflected on my achievement for as long as it took to shuffle another fifty yards to the refreshment table where there were cookies. Marathons are not for me, and it only took four tries and a combined twenty-eight hours on the trail to figure that out.

AT 8:00 A.M. on the Saturday closest to the autumnal equinox each September, several hundred runners and walkers assemble on the soccer field just outside the UAF Patty Center for the start of what has been called one of the toughest marathons in the country. Competitors in the Equinox Marathon cover the usual 26 miles, 385 yards, but also experience over 3,000 feet of cumulative elevation gain on the course that winds to the top of Ester Dome and back down again. (In fact, experienced runners may tell you it's the 3,000 feet of elevation loss coming down from the dome that really wears on the knees, shins, and ankles.)

The Equinox Marathon dates back to the early 1960s when founders Nat Goodhue, Gail Bakken, and Jim Mahaffey sought a way to protect the campus nature trails from the widespread construction then occurring at the university. They designed a course that begins and ends on campus and utilizes its extensive network of trails. Goodhue himself won the inaugural race in 1963.

But long distance running contests in Alaska have a much longer history than that.

In 1906 the Fraternal Order of Eagles in Nome built a new meeting hall complete with a circular running track. The relatively short loop measured only 165 feet around (32 laps to a mile), but its indoor location provided a diversion for Nome-ites through the long winter months.

In a gold rush town crazy for gambling, it's no surprise that running contests were soon organized. Locals wagered thousands of dollars on the races. They crowded the Eagles hall to cheer themselves hoarse as the competitors circled the track. These were contests of endurance, long-distance runs of up to fifty miles. The runners competed for thousands in cash prizes (plus whatever they or their proxies bet on themselves on the side).

The first hero of marathon running in Alaska was Jujiro Wada, a musher, prospector, and occasional restaurateur who came to the U.S. from his native Japan in 1892. Wada is best remembered today for his role in the Tanana gold rush and the founding of Fairbanks. Upon the discovery of gold in the region in 1902, Wada was dispatched to the Klondike to spread the news of the strike, resulting in hordes of men and women rushing the area and contributing to the overall settlement of Alaska's Interior.

Jujiro Wada (far right) and three other runners who competed in a 35-mile race in June 1907. Wada won $2,800 in prize money for his first place finish. His competitors are identified as (from left) Gonnet, Burman, and Sullivan. WADA JUJIRO KENSHO-KAI

By 1907 Wada found himself in Nome and, facing mounting personal debts, entered marathon races as a way of making money. He won his first fifty-mile race in early March with a time of just under eight hours—a pace of roughly nine and a half minutes per mile—then won another fifty-miler a few weeks later in near-identical time. His confidence buoyed by these successes, Wada (along with his fellow Japanese expatriates) began betting heavily on himself. For finishing first in a thirty-five-mile race that summer Wada took home $2,800 in prize money and who knows how much more in gambling winnings.

"The competitors entered in the twenty-five mile race...are all in perfect physical condition," stated the *Nome Gold Digger* before a May

1907 contest. "It is morally certain that the pace will be a hot one from the jump," the paper continued, "and any man who leaves the track will have little chance of picking up lost ground."

Marathon fever quickly spread to Fairbanks and Dawson City, where Wada again consistently finished in the money. Other top contenders in the races included Scotty Allen and H.M. Huber, both champion dog mushers as well.

Many of the top marathoners were mushers who also competed in long-distance dog races. The arduous work on the trail certainly prepared the men physically for marathon running, while countless hours standing on the sled's runners attuned them mentally for the challenge of running in circles for hours at a time. It was not uncommon for mushers to compete in long-distance dog races, such as the 400-mile All Alaska Sweepstakes from Nome to Candle and back, then enter a human-powered marathon a few days later.

Marathons in Alaska today are no longer gambling affairs, though a few side bets among friends are probably common. A $200 prize awaits any Equinox runner who breaks the course record in either the men's or women's divisions, but most runners participate only for the sense of accomplishment, the exhilaration of what is usually a beautiful autumn day on the trails, and the pride in receiving an Equinox patch, presented to all runners who finish the grueling race in under ten hours.

an
APOLOGETIC
DON

8

❖❖❖❖❖

Don Young is a paradox. Put him before a group of reporters or in a Congressional hearing where someone expresses a viewpoint he dislikes, and he is the very definition of the rude, obnoxious, ill-mannered politician. But ask anyone who has met with him informally in his office or bumped into him on the sidewalk and they'll tell you he is capable of great warmth and humor. I once passed by the Congressman in the cheese aisle at the supermarket and made a comment to the effect that I favored environmental preservation over rampant oil development—"Keep the Arctic Refuge wild!" were my exact words—and he laughed and said, "Oh no!" in a manner that was surprisingly jovial. It's just too bad that 90 percent of the time we get the other Don Young. This October 2007 column ends with a prediction that Young would face a tough re-election fight in 2008. He did. He still won.

In a closed-door meeting of House Republicans in mid-2007, Don Young rose and did something remarkable, something out of character for our notoriously hot-tempered Congressman: He apologized.

Two weeks earlier during a budget debate on the House floor, Young had lashed out at a fellow Republican who questioned $33 million in education funds tagged for Alaska. "Those who bite me," thundered Young, "will be bitten back." For a Congressman known to wave oosiks around during committee hearings and clamp a wolf trap on his own arm to make a point, junior members of the House could be forgiven for taking Young's ostensibly metaphorical words literally. In acknowledging that he "probably went overboard," Young apologized to colleagues and pledged to keep his temper in check for the sake of party unity.

If that sentiment sounds in any way familiar, it's because we've heard it all before from our Congressman. It was a well-timed apology in the 1992 election that saved Young's political career. That year, when he was a ten-term incumbent, Young faced the race of his life. His challenger was John Devens, the former mayor of Valdez who had won plaudits for his leadership following the Exxon Valdez spill. In many ways, however, Young's real opponent by that stage of his career was himself.

During his first two decades in Congress, Young developed a reputation for being prickly and openly hostile toward anyone who dared to disagree with him. He berated witnesses testifying before his committees until they cried, was known to bring hunting knives to committee hearings (drawing one out on at least one occasion), and once barked to a fellow Congressman, "Don't point your pencil at me or I'll shove it up your you-know-what."

After twenty years of this type of behavior Alaskans had had enough. Statewide polls showed Young with a 54 percent unfavorable rating. When asked about his performance in Congress, a combined 72 percent of respondents rated it as "only fair" or "poor." Just over a month before the election, polls showed Young a whopping 20 points behind Devens.

Clearly the Congressman needed a masterstroke to win back the affection of Alaskans.

It came in the form of what Young called his "mea culpa" TV commercial. "I want to talk to you about something that's difficult for me—my own shortcomings," Young said looking directly into the camera. "It's painfully clear to me that many feel I'm abrasive and arrogant, and I won't disagree. I have made some mistakes and I am sorry."

Within days of airing the TV spot, Young's numbers began to climb. In interviews and campaign appearances, a contrite Young promised Alaskans he'd do better. By Election Day the race was a dead heat. Early returns favored Devens, but Young pulled ahead and ultimately retained his seat by a margin of just 9,000 votes.

The remorse Young displayed in the campaign lasted only through Election Day and dissipated shortly thereafter. In the ensuing years, Young went back to his old habits. He has given the middle finger to reporters who dared question his actions, suggested that members of environmental groups are Communists who don't deserve to live in this country, and, in perhaps his most infamous outburst ever, used the word "buttf---ing" in a speech at a Fairbanks high school. (Forgive me for not providing the context for that remark—but really, under what circumstances would such language be acceptable?)

It appears in this current election cycle that Young may be in trouble again. In addition to an unpleasant disposition, his list of shortcomings now includes ties to former VECO chief Bill Allen and equally disgraced lobbyist Jack Abramoff, as well as allegations he inserted earmarks into a House transportation bill in return for campaign contributions. Unlike most previous elections where the Democrats put up only a token candidate against Young, this time both the state and national party have indicated their intent to field a prominent challenger and attempt to unseat the now 18-term incumbent.

If history is any guide, an attempt by Young to apologize his way out of this jam may depend more on his poll numbers a month before Election Day than any actual feelings of remorse.

NO
BLUSHING
HERE

A friend who serves on the Fairbanks Borough Assembly once told me that for any ordinance or resolution up for public comment, those citizens opposed to it nearly always outnumber any supporters in the assembly chambers, often by a significant margin. Supporters, secure in the knowledge the assembly is doing the right thing, are inclined to stay home. Dragging yourself to a public hearing is always easier when you're mad as hell! And when several dozen people all wearing red t-shirts show up at a public hearing, you can guess which side they're on.

OPPONENTS OF A Fairbanks City Council proposal to increase taxes on alcohol sales did more than show up in force at a November 2007 public hearing on the matter—they color-coordinated their outfits.

"WEAR RED to show your outrage!" proclaimed a half-page newspaper ad encouraging citizens to send a color-coded message to the mayor and council members. Sure enough, dozens of crimson-clad anti-tax activists packed the council chambers the following night and killed the measure.

Such a display would have been unthinkable just a generation ago.

There was a time when the term Red—a godless commie—was one of the worst epithets imaginable. Being called a pinko was almost worse.

At least full-fledged, card-carrying Reds stood by their convictions; pinkos only sympathized with the cause and hid their true feelings, so they were both commies and cowards.

No campaign in this country would have dared exhort its followers to appear publicly wearing either color. Yet roughly a decade ago, something changed. Nationwide and throughout Alaska, the political right began adopting red as the color of conservatism.

To wit: At a National Park Service hearing in 1998, held to collect public comment on a proposal prohibiting snowmachines from the interior of Denali Park, a couple hundred snow-go enthusiasts showed up wearing armbands of pink surveyor's tape. Maybe Samson's Hardware was just sold out of the other colors of tape that day—but had this hearing taken place two decades earlier during the ANILCA deliberations (where the Denali snowmachine regulations originated, by the way) you can bet no self-respecting rider would show up in any shade of pink or red. Those colors were reserved for Messrs. Carter, Udall, Seiberling, and their comrades who wanted to lock up Alaska.

The apotheosis of the color's newfound acceptance in local conservative circles came in 2005 with the "Save Eielson" campaign, an effort led by the conservative business establishment of Fairbanks to convince the Pentagon to keep the Air Force base open. The campaign's ubiquitous red t-shirts were a common sight that summer as everyone from local school-kids to our congressional delegation demonstrated their patriotic bona fides by donning a color that a generation ago would have gotten them ostracized.

So what happened? Why the switch?

Richard Nixon—the worst McCarthyite of them all, a man whose entire political career was founded on red-baiting—began the unraveling when he visited China, thereby diminishing the potency of "Red" as an insult. The collapse of the Soviet Union and the end of the Cold War then fully rendered the term obsolete.

The most significant factor in the color's ascendancy, however, was an otherwise innocuous decision by the major television networks in their news coverage of the 2000 election. For the first time in the history of televised news, every network used the same color scheme on its electoral maps: blue for the Democrats, red for the Republicans. The image not only represented the sharply divided electorate, but also became an icon for each party's respective political viewpoints.

Suddenly no conservative in the land saw any shame in the color red.

MAIL-ORDER
MATRIMONY

10

•••••

This column ran in the January 2008 edition of The Ester
Republic. *The following month another columnist, Neal
Matson, responded with the story of how he met Lisa, his
Filipina wife, via international mail and extolled the virtues
of dating by correspondence: "It is easier to communicate with
written words than on a face-to-face date. It is easier to be
honest, it is less expensive, doesn't require a fancy wardrobe
or even shaving, and one can end a relationship that is going
nowhere much more gently. True, there is no physical contact
or pheromonic influence, but that just makes the eventual in-
person meeting more intense. Within the few hours of my bride
meeting me at the airport it was as if we had known each other
all of our lives. We had been corresponding for nearly a year
and decided to get married as soon as possible." Neal and Lisa
have been married for twenty-nine years.*

A RECENT STUDY by the U.S. Census Bureau confirmed what we've known
all along—what Alaskans have taken for granted for the past hundred
years, in fact—that men outnumber women here in the North. The study
found that in 2006 there were 107 men in Alaska for every 100 women,
the most lopsided ratio in the U.S. (The District of Columbia is at the
other end of the scale with only 88 men per 100 women.)

Wedding dinner of Mr. and Mrs. Peter E. Kern of Skagway, probably in the early 1900s. The grinning woman seated next to the bride is identified as Mrs. Keith, the "match maker." J. BERNARD MOORE FAMILY PAPERS, ALBUM #1, UAF-1976-35-86, ALASKA AND POLAR REGIONS, RASMUSON LIBRARY, UNIVERSITY OF ALASKA FAIRBANKS

For single women in Alaska, then, it is more or less a buyer's market.

A century ago, of course, the situation in the Interior was much more extreme. The dearth of women inspired one local bachelor in the spring of 1908 to write anonymously to the Seattle Chamber of Commerce:

> *Fairbanks is the newest frontier town in the United States....*
> *I think if you people would advertise our wants in districts*
> *where there is a surplus of women...you would be doing us a*
> *favor that couldn't be measured from a monetary standard.*

The response was immediate. According to an article in the July 19, 1908, edition of the *Fairbanks Sunday Times*, an "avalanche" of letters arrived at the newspaper's office.

"As I am anxious to marry some good man," wrote Helen Hill of Spokane, a woman by her own description healthy, young, and good-looking, "I depend on your good nature to give my name and address to three or four good, well-to-do men, no matter what business they are in as long as they are reliable."

May Stoner and Gladys Bair, both of Seattle, wrote the Fairbanks paper seeking "husbands that are kind-hearted and have a pocketbook that holds enough for two."

Hattie Lovejoy of San Jose, California, wrote on behalf of a young woman (her daughter, perhaps?) "who has every qualification to make a good wife. She is honorable, cheerful, a good cook."

The Fairbanks paper encouraged the local men to get busy at once and answer the letters.

In her book *Romance on a Global Stage*, anthropologist Nicole Constable explores the phenomenon of so-called mail-order marriages between American men and Asian women. Her findings in that context may tell us something about those early days in Fairbanks.

Constable writes that while such mail-order marriages are nearly always couched in terms of "romantic love," they are also linked to the market forces of the respective societies in which they take place. Prospective husbands, the author notes, often object to the notion that brides willing to relocate might be looking for a free lunch. Such an assertion reduces what is ostensibly an intimate personal connection to a simple market transaction.

The women, on the other hand, prove more able to acknowledge the economic considerations at play. Note how the lonely bachelor's letter downplays the "monetary standard," while the women who replied have the capacity of the men's pocketbooks squarely in focus. Put another way—and all stereotypes about gold diggers aside—no prospective marriage partner is going to migrate to an economically depressed territory, no matter the number of eligible matches.

The *Fairbanks Sunday Times* grasped this phenomenon a century ago in a sentiment that rings true today:

> *Alaskans are much sought after as husbands. Why? Perhaps it is because they are so closely associated with the golden treasures of the fabled Northland; perhaps it is because they are of an adventuresome spirit, men who have shaken off the outside conventionality to do and dare, in a country noted for its extreme rigors and rich rewards, or possibly because Alaskans, as a rule, make a noise like ready money outside.*

Men and women have perennially immigrated to Alaska for its many economic opportunities. If the prospect of money brought them here, why shouldn't their potential spouses have similar ambitions?

SOME
OLD
YOUNG
HISTORY

•••••

Shortly after this column appeared in February 2008, Sean Parnell, then the state's lieutenant governor, announced he would challenge Congressman Don Young in the Republican primary. Nicknamed "Captain Zero" for his less than magnetic personality, Parnell lived up to the moniker by running an uninspired campaign. Young squeaked by with a 304-vote primary victory. Statewide polls then showed Young trailing his Democrat opponent, Ethan Berkowitz, by as many as 16 points. It appeared Young's career in the House was nearing its end. Incredibly, Young proved every pre-election poll dead wrong and defeated Berkowitz by a comfortable margin.

DON YOUNG HAS served in Congress as Alaska's lone representative since 1973. The electoral advantage of this incumbency is hard to overstate. Any candidate looking to unseat Young has to not only match both his statewide name recognition and inestimable fundraising apparatus, but somehow convince voters to sack an eighteen-term incumbent, whose seniority in Congress has granted him the ability to direct millions in federal funds back to Alaska, and replace him with a rookie legislator.

Such prospective challengers looking to use history as a guide might ask: How did Don Young himself do it some thirty-six years ago when he was the challenger looking to unseat a popular incumbent?

In 1972 Alaska was represented in Congress by Democrat Nick Begich. Though still in only his first term, Begich was popular throughout the state, particularly in his hometown of Anchorage and in the Bush—two key voting blocs that together represented a majority of the electorate. His re-election was all but guaranteed.

The Republican Party chose as its candidate a schoolteacher and state legislator from Fort Yukon named Don Young. Despite being viewed as a token nominee who stood little chance against Begich, Young embarked on an aggressive campaign. He first sought to differentiate himself from Begich the only way an unknown, unproven candidate possibly can: by aligning himself with a higher profile candidate of the same party. There was no more well-known Republican in 1972 than the one running for his second term as president.

"Richard Nixon will be elected in November," Young told the Fairbanks Chamber of Commerce seven weeks before the election, "and when he is, the keys to the restroom will go to me, not Nick Begich." That Congress was safely in the hands of the Democrats—where Young would be a freshman minority member with no keys whatsoever save those to his own office—went unmentioned by the Republican from Fort Yukon.

Young also challenged the incumbent to a series of debates. By mid-September, Young expressed frustration that Begich had not returned from Washington to bring important issues before the public. The congressman was failing in his duties as a public official, said Young, by not coming home to speak directly to Alaskans.

Begich accepted Young's challenge, but noted the debates would have to wait until after Congress adjourned. With Alaska-related legislation still on the table, Begich countered he would be doing Alaskans a disservice by dashing home in search of campaign headlines. (The very same scene played out in the Senate race that year, where Democrat Gene Guess criticized Republican incumbent Ted Stevens for remaining in Washington and avoiding debates. Stevens's response was identical to that of Begich.)

Congressman Nick Begich U.S. GOVERNMENT
PRINTING OFFICE

By the time of the first Begich-Young debate on October 6, the challenger was doing about as well as could be expected. Young had drawn a clear distinction between himself and the congressman in the context of the national political scene, and had taken advantage of Begich's lengthy absence from the campaign trail to hammer what Young called his "anti-business" voting record. Young also sought to link Begich with George McGovern, the floundering Democratic presidential candidate, who had refused to explicitly support the trans-Alaska oil pipeline.

Their first debate, held at the Traveler's Inn in Fairbanks, offered a study in contrasts. The incumbent put forth his record, noting his work on the Alaska Native Claims Settlement Act and the fact he had made the floor vote on 884 of 888 bills his first term. The challenger, with no such record to speak of, again played the Nixon card and suggested he was the one to "straighten out the crazy ideas people have about Alaska."

The following week, a plane carrying Begich, House Majority Leader Hale Boggs of Louisiana, and two others disappeared over the Gulf of Alaska. Although Begich was missing and presumed dead, his name remained on the ballot. Young toned down his campaign, but urged Alaskans not to let the state's lone seat remain vacant when Congress reconvened in January.

An extensive search failed to locate the plane's wreckage or evidence of the missing passengers. A judge declared Begich legally deceased—but not before the incumbent defeated Young by 12,000 votes. The state scheduled a special election for March 1973 to fill his open seat.

Alaska Democrats considered nominating Pegge Begich, Nick's widow, but ultimately decided on Emil Notti, a 39-year old Koyukuk native and former party chairman. The Republicans stuck with Young, who suddenly found himself the candidate with greater name recognition (in urban areas at least).

With both candidates running essentially as challengers, neither was in a position to claim legislative experience or cite accomplishments of the type usually found on an incumbent's resume. Instead, the two men showcased their respective party affiliations and supposed access to the real seats of power in Washington. Young reminded voters about the Republican in the White House (Nixon had been re-elected in a landslide) while Notti emphasized his connections to the Democratic leadership in the House, the place where he noted all legislation, such as an Alaska pipeline bill, would actually move.

Notti polled well in the Bush, but Young swept the urban areas (even turning what had been a 1,300-vote deficit to Begich in Fairbanks three months before into a 1,100-vote surplus) and won the special election. He hasn't looked back since.

Young's campaign strategy in 1972 bears almost no resemblance to his re-election runs of late. When challenging the incumbent Begich, and later going head-to-head with Notti for the open seat, Young had to prove himself worthy of Alaskans' votes and he worked his tail off. His most recent campaigns, however, have consisted almost entirely of generic TV, radio, and newspaper ads that are devoid of any issues or policy statements. He has made few public appearances and, in 2006, spurned every debate invitation from Democrat Diane Benson, even going so far as to cancel a speaking engagement when he learned she would be appearing at the same event. The very things he accused Begich of in 1972—hiding out in Washington, dodging debates, failing to bring issues before the voters—have become hallmarks of Young's campaigns.

With Democrats controlling Congress and poised to take back the White House, any future challenger for Young's seat may choose to employ the "keys to the restroom" strategy he himself once used. As for the incumbent, with a long list of accomplishments now on his resume he is capable of running a different type of campaign, and he remains a formidable candidate.

CLEARY
SUMMIT
BURNING

◆◆◆◆◆

The destruction of the Cleary Summit ski lodge by fire was a real tragedy—the loss of a Fairbanks cultural landmark, as this column describes—but it's hard not to be amused by the actions of the hapless individual suspected of starting the fire. A few hours after the blaze, with the lodge a smoldering ruin and the scene crawling with Alaska State Troopers, the young man returned and attempted to retrieve his pickup. Standing in the snow with his shoes burnt through, his socks charred, smoke wafting from his person, and without any explanation for why his truck was there or where he'd been the last few hours, the man denied knowing anything about the fire. Troopers arrested him. One other note: The Alaska Lost Ski Areas Project (www. alsap.org) is a remarkable collection of historical information, personal accounts, and photographs that proved invaluable in the research for this column.

WHEN FIRE DESTROYED the old Cleary Summit ski lodge on January 29, 2008, it was another chapter closed in the book of local ski areas lost to history.

Started on a shoestring budget in 1949 by Bob and Sylvia McCann and Link Imeson, the Cleary Summit Ski Area had no lift of any kind that first winter, so skiers had to hoof it up the slope. In time the ski area

Bob McCann hands skis to a young man at Cleary Summit Lodge in the 1960s. BEVINNE MORSE

featured two rope tows, a T-bar lift, and a platter pull for beginners on the bunny hill. The Steese Highway bisected the upper and lower slopes, but skiers remained free to glide straight across since the road wasn't plowed that far in.

Fire was no stranger to Cleary Summit. The first lodge burned under suspicious circumstances in May 1952. McCann and Imeson had been wiring the lodge for electricity—but the generator was not yet operational. A cause of the fire was never determined.

The lodge was sufficiently insured to allow McCann and Imeson to rebuild, but the second lodge also burned to the ground. Fumes from a linoleum floor McCann was pouring ignited and, with the only fire service over twenty miles away in Fairbanks, he could only watch as the structure immolated. Still a third lodge was destroyed when a carelessly tossed cigarette ignited a generously stuffed and upholstered sofa.

In 1960, the McCanns built a magnificent three-story, A-frame chalet with bright green, yellow, and orange siding. The 7,000-square-foot lodge remained in use until the ski area closed in 1993. Abandoned since then, the lodge fell into disrepair and became a target for vandalism. Investigators believe the January fire that destroyed the lodge started when a local man, whose truck had broken down on the Steese a short walk from the lodge, took refuge there and attempted to start a fire for warmth.

(Interestingly—at least for the antiquity-minded who appreciate historical anniversaries—the lodge fire occurred almost exactly 100 years after an inferno that leveled the whole town of Cleary. In November 1907 crossed wires at the Totem Saloon began "spitting fire," according to newspaper accounts. Buffeted by strong winds, the resultant blaze tore through the Cleary business section. Dozens of buildings were destroyed.)

Closer to Ester, the Ullrhaven Ski Area operated on Ester Dome in the late 1950s and early 1960s. Named for Ullr, a Scandinavian god of skiing and bowhunting, Ullrhaven was started by University of Alaska students and featured a hexagonal lodge made of logs and two rope tows powered by an old pickup engine. The use of university land and student activity fees to fund the enterprise caused Bob McCann of Cleary Summit to complain to Governor Bill Egan about the university competing with the private sector. Ullrhaven closed shortly thereafter.

Even then, students didn't have far to go to hit the slopes. A simple rope tow operated for decades on the University Ski Hill (just behind where the Student Rec Center stands today). The hill also included a 100-foot ski jump named for Ivar Skarland. The rope tow was dismantled in the early 1980s, and the ski hill officially closed following a fatal sledding accident in 1988. (The chainlink fences you see criss-crossing the hill today are an end result of a lawsuit filed against the university by the family of the deceased student.)

In all, the Fairbanks area has enjoyed no less than a dozen ski areas, jumps, and trail systems throughout its history. Many of these started when a dedicated group of skiing enthusiasts cleared a slope and jury-rigged a lift system comprised of ropes, pulleys, and an old engine. The history of these ski areas reminds us of a time when folks created their own entertainment. As one ski jumper from 1950s Fairbanks put it, "There wasn't much else for recreation."

the
STATE
of
OIL

• • • • •

Alaska's relationship with the oil industry goes back more than a century. The first large-scale commercial oil development in Alaska began at Swanson River in 1957. The strike at Prudhoe Bay a decade later solidified the bond between the state and the largest oil companies in the world. In many ways, however, the story of oil is not about Exxon, ARCO, BP, Chevron, and the other multinationals, but rather everyday Alaskans who found themselves in a position to steer the course of history. They were geologists, surveyors, elected officials, environmentalists, lawyers, and many others who played roles that were often wildly disproportionate to their standing in the power structure of the global oil game. They made these contributions because they cared and they stood up. In a place like Alaska that's often all it takes. The three-part series here includes some of those stories.

I. A WISE CHOICE

IN FEBRUARY 2008, oil companies eager to drill in the Chukchi Sea bid a record $2.7 billion at a lease sale in Anchorage.

Alaska's share of that bonanza? Zero.

The federal government holds leasing rights to offshore acreage and thus all revenue from the sale goes to Washington. State lawmakers are working to change that. Under a proposal in the State Legislature, Alaska would receive just over one-third of lease revenue for the Outer Continental Shelf.

Bill Wielechowski, an Anchorage Democrat and sponsor of the resolution, noted that Texas, Louisiana, Mississippi, and Alabama all receive royalties from oil leasing in the Gulf of Mexico. Ralph Samuels, a Republican House member from Anchorage, explained how revenue sharing would help offset the costs of oil workers and their families using state services such as roads, schools, and hospitals.

As legislators attempt to remedy this situation, it is worth remembering how close we came to similarly missing out on Prudhoe Bay. Were it not for the foresight of a handful of Alaskans—one state geologist in particular—that oil field too may have remained in the pocket of the federal government and been just another missed opportunity for the state.

Under the statehood act of 1959, Congress authorized Alaska to select just over 100 million acres of unappropriated public land. For a new state with few other sources of revenue, the immediate priority was to select lands that could be sold to the private sector for agriculture, homesteading, and other forms of development.

The Department of Natural Resources, however, took a broader view. The disposal of state land to private individuals served a valuable function, but the department also saw the wisdom in selecting large, even remote sections with resource potential. Such investments might provide sizeable long-term returns to the state.

Tom Marshall, a geologist and land selection officer at DNR, pored over maps looking for such parcels. He though he'd found one on the North Slope, a wedge of land sandwiched between the Arctic National Wildlife Range to the east and the Naval Petroleum Reserve No. 4 to the west (both federal lands).

That oil and gas could be found on the North Slope was well known. Surface seeps had been discovered as far back as the mid-nineteenth century. Anecdotal evidence suggested Alaska Natives had for centuries burned petroleum-laden chunks of sod. As early as 1924 the U.S. Geo-

State Geologist Tom Marshall catalogues rock cores and cuttings from Alaskan oil wells in 1964. ANCHORAGE DAILY NEWS/MCT/LANDOV

logical Survey prepared maps and topographic charts of the region. From 1944 to 1953 the Survey conducted seismic testing and drilled exploratory wells in the foothills of the Brooks Range.

Though he possessed few charts of the coastal plain to the north, Marshall was impressed with the known geology and its potential for oil and gas reservoirs. The fact that a handful of oil companies had survey crews on the North Slope further convinced Marshall the area was worth something. He selected some two million acres, an area that included a small, unremarkable cove called Prudhoe Bay.

At the same time, two other Alaskans were on the ground exploring the coastal plain. Gil Mull and Gar Pessel, geologists working for the Richfield Oil Company (later ARCO), studied the Sagavanirktok River region. Their favorable reports to Richfield's Los Angeles headquarters— Mull and Pessel excitedly noted the "petroliferous nature of these sands"— convinced the company to invest in further North Slope exploration.

Alaska held an oil and gas lease sale for its newly selected North Slope lands in 1964. Richfield, by then in a 50-50 partnership with Humble Oil (later Exxon), bid aggressively and secured significant acreage. The state took in $12 million, a huge sum at that time. Marshall's selection would have been worth the trouble even if that was the end of it—even if no oil had been found, not a single drop, and not another penny in leases or royalties had accrued to the state. The administrative costs for title to the North Slope land totaled just $40,000, which the lease sale more than covered.

The big payoff, of course, came five years later following the Prudhoe strike. Alaska held another lease sale in 1969 that generated $900 million and ushered in a brand new era in our state's history.

For a select group of Fairbanksans, however, the 1969 lease sale was bittersweet. What was good for the state collectively proved unfortunate for them personally. These men and women also held North Slope leases, secured before most people had ever heard of Prudhoe Bay and which now stood to make them all millionaires. Until the state revoked the leases, that is.

II. THE LITTLE GUYS AND THE BIG FELLOWS

In September 1969, the State of Alaska held an oil and gas lease sale in which it auctioned drilling rights on half a million acres of the most promising oil-rich lands at Prudhoe Bay. The sale raised $900 million and catapulted Alaska into a new era of fabulous oil wealth. For roughly one hundred Alaskans, however, the sale held an altogether different meaning. It was the day they watched their personal fortunes slip away.

Governor Keith Miller (holding microphone) and Resources Commissioner Tom Kelly (far right) at the conclusion of the Prudhoe Bay lease sale in September 1969. WARD WELLS, WARD WELLS COLLECTION, ANCHORAGE MUSEUM, B83.91. S4794.6

Prior to statehood, when the federal government controlled nearly all the land in Alaska, the Bureau of Land Management typically employed a policy of non-competitive leasing of natural resources. Rather than auction development rights to the highest bidder, the government simply granted leases on a first-come, first-served basis to anyone who filed an application and paid a modest recording fee.

After 1959, however, Alaska began selecting some 100 million acres of land granted under the statehood act. By state law, resource development rights on such lands were to be conveyed only by competitive bid at publicly announced lease sales.

Which leasing policy had standing in those early days was an open question. Did the state's policy of competitive bid take effect the moment land was selected? Or only after Washington officially transferred the title? And what did Interior Secretary Stewart Udall's 1966 land freeze mean for resource development?

Whatever the case, dozens of clever Alaskans knew that even by the mid-1960s you could secure oil leases just by filling out a form. These forward-thinking individuals kept a close eye on the oil companies and the state's land selection office. When attention turned to a two million-acre parcel on the North Slope near a place called Prudhoe Bay, they marched into the lands office and staked claim to the open adjacent acreage.

Upon discovery of the mammoth oil field a few years later, these men and women found themselves sitting on leases worth millions. None had any intention of drilling for oil themselves (not that they had the financial backing or technical expertise to do so anyway) but rather looked to sublet the leases to the major oil companies while retaining an interest in future royalties.

The state had other plans, however.

In January 1969, while planning for the big lease sale later that year, resources commissioner Tom Kelly announced the reclassification of the now appropriated state land. Oil and gas leases would be granted only by competitive bid. "There is no question," said Kelly, "that leasing the entire area competitively will result in receiving considerably more revenue over non-competitive leasing." His action effectively swept the little guys off the map.

The Fairbanks leaseholders were hot. The group, led by Cliff Burglin, Bill Stroecker, and Bill Waugaman, called a public meeting at the Eagles Hall to air their grievances. "It looks as though Tom Kelly is taking the land away from the people of Alaska and selling it to the big fellows," said Waugaman, a miner and former legislator.

The group claimed the state not only had a legal obligation to honor the leases, but that Alaska would be better off with local investors who could be counted upon to pump every dollar of oil profits back into the local economy. The oil companies, they argued, would take their profits out of the state. Kelly countered that his oath of office required him to act in the best interests of the entire state. Honoring the non-competitive leases would cost Alaska millions in lost lease revenue. The reclassification stood.

Although one might have expected strongly libertarian Alaskans to empathize with the aggrieved oil speculators, Kelly's position ruled the day. The sale of leases at Prudhoe Bay promised to be the state's ticket to riches, and Alaskans supported efforts to wring every penny from the once-in-a-lifetime opportunity.

III. PAY THE RENT

A small group of protesters gathered in freezing temperatures outside the Loussac Library in Anchorage in February 2008. Inside was a Chukchi Sea oil and gas lease sale that ultimately raised a record $2.7 billion from Shell and other companies eager to drill the Outer Continental Shelf. The protesters—environmentalists and Alaska Natives from Point Hope and Barrow—feared the effects offshore oil development might have on wild-life, including polar bears and whales. They also doubted the industry's ability to prevent and clean up oil spills. The village of Point Hope and several environmental groups have challenged the lease sale in court.

Environmentalists protesting oil development is old hat. But the presence of Alaska Natives at the lease sale calls to mind a similar protest nearly four decades ago.

The Prudhoe Bay lease sale took place in September 1969 at the Sydney Laurence Auditorium in downtown Anchorage. A dozen Alaska Natives marched on the sidewalks outside holding signs that read, "Eskimos Own North Slope," "$2,000,000,000 Native Land Robbery," and "Bad Deal at Tom Kelly's Trading Post" (Kelly was the state's resources commissioner at the time).

The group was led by Charlie "Etok" Edwardsen, Jr., an Eskimo from Barrow whose militant stance on Native rights often put him at odds with the more conservative, established groups, such as the Alaska Federation of Natives. As told by Hugh Gregory Gallagher in *Etok: A Story of Eskimo Power*, the young Native leader did not hold back: "Today's lease sale is perpetration of economic genocide on a Native minority."

At issue was the true ownership of the North Slope. The State of Alaska had selected Prudhoe Bay as part of its land allotment under the statehood act, but indigenous people could claim aboriginal title to lands they had inhabited for thousands of years. "How can the white man sell our land," asked Edwardsen, "when they do not own it?"

Eben Hopson, another Native leader from Barrow, was less fanatical than Edwardsen but expressed similar frustration: "Are we to assume that so long as their [non-Natives] pockets are full of green stuff...everything is fine? What manner of conscience is this?"

Alaska Natives had been pushing for a land claims settlement for decades. The idea met firm resistance from federal and state officials—until the Prudhoe strike. Natives found themselves with sudden bargaining power when it became clear that oil development could not proceed until the lands issue was settled. In December 1971, Congress passed the Alaska Native Claims Settlement Act (ANCSA), which organized Natives into regional and village corporations and allocated to them 40 million acres of land and nearly $1 billion.

The Edwardsen protest had little effect on these developments. AFN chairman Don Wright noted that no official Native organization supported his effort. Edwardsen was able to convince only a dozen followers to join him outside the lease sale. But the event was covered by U.S. and international press, and in Edwardsen the media found an outspoken, articulate man who could always be counted on for a good contrarian quote. (A few years later at a Congressional hearing on North Slope oil production, Edwardsen shouted to reporters, "If the pigs want to use our land, then the pigs must pay the rent!")

In this, Edwardsen filled the same niche for Alaska Natives that David Brower, the fiery and antagonistic head of Friends of the Earth, did for the environmentalists. Both men, it was said, did their respective causes a favor by making everyone else seem so damn reasonable.

THE AUSTRIAN SKIER,
THE GERMAN ARCHAEOLOGIST,
and
THE COUNTRY THAT SEES
SUBVERSIVES EVERYWHERE

•••••

At the time this column was printed in July 2008, Reinhard Neuhauser was back in Austria. No one would have blamed him had he decided to stay there permanently. His abominable treatment by U.S. border agents six months earlier, as this column describes, was infuriating then and remains an embarrassment today. Neuhauser's attachment to Alaska is strong, however, and he returned to Fairbanks that October. He told me that immigration officials in Anchorage again took him to the back office and triple-checked his papers, a process likely to be repeated every time he enters the U.S. "It was an uncomfortable feeling," he said.

BY NOW THE story of Reinhard Neuhauser is well known. The UAA graduate, local ski instructor, and six-year Alaska resident was returning from his native Austria in January 2008 to accept a position with the Fairbanks Economic Development Corporation when immigration officials detained him Seattle. After being informed he was holding the wrong type of visa—a mistake for which the U.S. consulate in Vienna is apparently responsible—Neuhauser was interrogated, strip searched, jailed overnight (where he was not allowed to sleep for more than a few minutes), and put back on a plane for Austria at his own expense. It is uncertain whether he will ever be allowed back in the U.S.—assuming he even wants to return.

This type of Kafkaesque treatment of foreign-born Alaska residents might sound like only a post-9/11 phenomenon. Sadly, it's not.

In the fall of 1941, Otto Geist was preparing to travel to New York. As in most years, the archaeologist had spent the spring and summer traveling all over northern Alaska collecting Pleistocene-era fossils, mostly mammoth and bison bones, which he now intended to deliver to museums and laboratories on the east coast. Despite having almost no formal academic training, Geist had established himself as a pioneer of Alaska archaeology and paleontology. He initiated ethnographic studies of Alaska Native cultures and amassed an unrivaled collection of native artifacts and natural history specimens, accomplishments for which he would one day be awarded an honorary doctorate from the University of Alaska.

But in late 1941 he was just a German-born immigrant who had the misfortune of planning a trip Outside the same week the Japanese bombed Pearl Harbor.

Alaskans were jittery as they wondered whether Japan would bomb Juneau or Anchorage next. Towns along the coast eagerly enforced blackouts. It was not uncommon to see men with guns cruising the streets of Anchorage late at night.

As told by journalist Charles Keim in *Aghvook, White Eskimo*, it was in this atmosphere of fear that suspicions arose about the true nature of Geist's trip. While in Anchorage for a few days waiting for a train, Geist stayed with friends and kept a low profile. In Seward he boarded a steamer along with another German who had been on a hunting trip in Alaska. The ship was stopped repeatedly by patrols looking for aliens, but, amazingly, both men managed to reach Seattle unmolested.

On his return trip in the spring of 1942, Geist was detained in Seattle for three hours while officials examined his papers. Only when prominent Alaska officials traveling on the same steamer vouched for him was Geist allowed to travel. Back in Fairbanks, an army officer ran into Geist and, stunned to see the suspected double-agent in the flesh, blurted out, "We had orders to stop you. We heard that you were trying to take a great many maps out of Alaska."

Major Otto Geist, Quartermaster in the Alaska Territorial Guard, in Nome, Alaska in the 1940s. CLARENCE L. ANDREWS PHOTOGRAPH COLLECTION, P45-1317, ALASKA STATE LIBRARY

Geist had put up with such nonsense before. In 1918 he was a naturalized citizen serving in the U.S. Army when his commanding officer learned he'd been in the German infantry as a teenager a decade earlier. The officer stripped Geist of his rank and assigned soldiers from his own company to keep 24-hour watch on the man suddenly suspected of being a spy. At the time, Geist was caring for soldiers dying in the influenza epidemic—a duty one could hardly characterize as a potential intelligence breach—and his guards privately apologized for their xenophobic officer.

Geist and Neuhauser are alike in another respect. Their treatment is all the more galling when one considers the many selfless contributions both made to Alaska. Neuhauser volunteered as a ski instructor in Fairbanks, once bringing a group of local kids to Austria for an alpine skiing camp. As one close friend put it, "He has done more for Alaska in six years than most have probably done in a lifetime."

By the same token, Geist's record of public service in Alaska is beyond stellar. During World War II, Geist helped organize the Alaska Territorial Guard, an all-volunteer reconnaissance and defense force comprised mainly of Alaska Natives. ATG officials wanted leaders who understood village life and had the respect of Natives. Geist was the perfect choice.

Though the ATG was never called upon for much more than marksmanship training, it left a remarkable legacy. The campaign marked the first time that the federal government engaged Alaska Natives in an official, non-paternalistic capacity. No one showed up in the villages to proselytize or send the children off to boarding schools. Instead the military came to distribute rifles and ask the Natives for help in defending Alaska.

One can hardly gauge the lasting impact of this simple action. By treating the men as equals, Geist and the ATG created a territory-wide social and political structure that empowered Natives for decades afterward. Historians cite the ATG as a key factor in the later political emergence of Alaska Natives.

Now imagine how history might be different had Geist been kicked out of Alaska by any of the suspicious, small-minded men who suspected him of stealing maps.

One has to wonder what Neuhauser might have achieved for Alaska had we given him the chance.

the
OPPOSITION
POSITION

A simple statement of opposition by the commissioner of the U.S. Bureau of Fisheries in January 1916 might reasonably be called one of the first direct actions against Alaska statehood. James Wickersham, then Alaska's non-voting delegate to Congress, proposed that fish and wildlife management be transferred to the territory. In spiking the proposal, the aforementioned bureaucrat only strengthened Wickersham's resolve. He introduced the first Alaska statehood bill two months later and made fish and wildlife management a dominate plank of the statehood platform. From that moment until statehood was finally achieved in 1959, the arguments against statehood took many forms. This column, first printed in August 2008 on the fiftieth anniversary of the statehood vote, explores a few of those statements of opposition.

WHEN CONGRESS PASSED the Alaska Statehood Act in June 1958, both planned and spontaneous celebrations erupted across the territory. After decades of second-class territorial status, Alaska was finally a state.

Well, not quite.

President Eisenhower's signature on the bill notwithstanding, voters in Alaska still had to approve the act before it became official. On August 26, 1958, Alaskans went to the polls in the first statehood primary to decide, among other matters, whether to approve the statehood act. Not surprisingly, the proposition passed by a vote of 40,452 to 8,010.

No one ever seriously doubted the result, but the vote still begs the question: What about the eight thousand Alaskans who voted 'no'? Our collective commemoration of statehood has enshrined only those noble arguments in favor—economic self-determination, natural resource management, full political representation, and so on—but surely the anti-statehooders had their reasons as well.

In a single word—taxes.

"I wouldn't be caught dead voting for statehood," wrote Allen Diershaw of Fairbanks in a letter to the editor a few days before the primary. Diershaw didn't mind the handful of minor taxes he paid now, but he foresaw lots more under the new statehood bureaucracy: "Reason predicts another pile of bricks for the old donkey."

Al Anderson and Glenn Carrington of the Alaska Miners Association feared corporate taxes under statehood. They believed only the free flow of capital would spur the industrial development so badly needed in Alaska. It pained them to see Outside corporate interests "regarded as a parasite," they told Congress at a statehood hearing in 1945.

Robert DeArmond, a journalist who worked for a number of anti-statehood newspapers in the territory, agreed that taxing Outside industry would only drive it away, and that Alaska's small population was simply not prepared to pay the exorbitant costs of statehood on its own. "How much of an additional tax burden are the people willing to assume to pay the costs of state government," he wrote in 1950. "25 percent? 50 percent? 75 percent? 100 percent?"

Future governor Jay Hammond, while a federal game manager and wilderness guide in Naknek in the 1950s, also opposed statehood on the grounds that the territory simply wasn't prepared to support itself economically. Decades later Hammond would point to the financial dire straits of the immediate post-statehood era as evidence backing up his earlier claim. In Hammond's largely accurate view, only the infusion of federal relief funds after the 1964 earthquake and the Prudhoe Bay strike

Winton C. Arnold, former judge, lobbyist for the salmon packers, and face of the anti-statehood movement in the 1940s and 50s. ALASKA STATE LIBRARY PORTRAIT FILE, P01-1437, ALASKA STATE LIBRARY

four years later (an unbelievable windfall the scope of which was impossible to predict before statehood) saved the state.

Many sportsmen, though not explicitly against statehood, nevertheless feared whatever new system of game management statehood would bring. A.W. Boddy of the Alaska Sportsmens Council testified before Congress that wildlife management should remain with the feds no matter what since Alaskans were too politically immature to do it themselves.

Just three days before the statehood vote, Jack Boswell, president of the Tanana Valley Sportsmens Association and devoted statehood advocate, stirred up a minor kerfuffle when he called a meeting to which many anti-statehooders were invited. Boswell assured worried locals that the meeting was not a maneuver against the upcoming vote, but a good faith effort to include all viewpoints on the game management issue.

Some Alaskans qualified their opposition to statehood by saying it might make sense someday, just not now. Suspicion also ran high regarding the true motivation of the pro-statehooders. Many, including Hammond, believed their enthusiasm stemmed from a self-interested desire to hold public office—a claim borne out in part by the countless dozens of candidates who filed in that first primary. The obligatory "candidate questionnaire" section of the *Fairbanks Daily News-Miner* filled an entire section all on its own.

Under Cap Lathrop the *News-Miner* was stridently anti-statehood. Lathrop, the media and mining mogul famous as Alaska's first homegrown millionaire, opposed statehood for the aforementioned economic reasons. Following his death in 1950, new owner and publisher C.W. Snedden turned the paper around and it became a solid editorial voice in favor of Alaska statehood.

In the days leading up to the 1958 primary, Snedden used his paper to dispel some of the "ridiculous rumors" then in circulation. It was believed, at least in some quarters, that statehood would make it illegal to own unprocessed gold and would result in legalized gambling, state-owned liquor stores, and easy divorce laws. The most pernicious rumor held that Alaska Natives would be forced onto reservations and limited to one square mile each for hunting and fishing. Regardless of how effectively Snedden debunked these myths, it seems likely that at least a few of the eight thousand votes against statehood were cast in the belief they were true.

For many Alaskans, the embodiment of the anti-statehood movement was Winton C. Arnold, a one-time magistrate from Ketchikan known by friend and foe alike as "Judge." As head lobbyist for the Seattle-based salmon canning industry, Arnold had managed and manipulated the territorial legislature to great effect, once allegedly leaning over the rail of the visitors' gallery to direct legislators how to vote.

The salmon packers resisted statehood for the local control (i.e., sustainable harvest quotas and abolition of fish traps) it would surely bring. But Arnold, always the star witness for the anti-statehooders at congressional hearings, was given to cite any number of arguments completely unrelated to fisheries.

At a Senate hearing in 1950, for example, Arnold protested that the statehood bill under consideration did not appropriately address state land selections and Alaska Native land claims. He was right. The section was fixed in the next statehood bill. A number of historians have pointed out the irony in Arnold's anti-statehood efforts. By repeatedly identifying the shortcomings of the Alaska bills, he essentially provided statehooders with a road map for fixing every problem. Each successive round with Judge Arnold, and there were many over the decades, resulted in better and better statehood bills—until one finally met with success in 1958.

WON'T GET FOOLED AGAIN!

◆◆◆◆◆

While writing this column on the state's protracted tug-of-war with Exxon over the Point Thomson leases, I was reminded of something longtime Fairbanks journalist Dermot Cole once said with regard to the always-proposed-but-never-built Alaska gas pipeline: "In thirty years as a reporter I've written more 'Gas Line Coming' headlines than anyone." Shortly after this column was published in September 2008, Tom Irwin, the state's resources commissioner who had previously threatened to revoke Exxon's leases at Point Thomson, reversed course and provisionally accepted the oil giant's development proposal. As of this writing in early 2011, two wells have been drilled with the first oil and gas scheduled to flow in 2014.

THE TIME IS apparently up for Exxon on Point Thomson.

After twenty-three development proposals and three decades of stalling on the undeveloped oil and gas field, the state is prepared to revoke Exxon's leases. How does the saying go? Fool me once shame on you, fool me twenty-three times…

On the surface it all seems so counterintuitive. Point Thomson contains proven petroleum reserves and developing the field would mean billions in profit for Exxon. So what's the hold-up? To a casual observer, the idea of an oil company intentionally delaying a project makes no sense.

But from an industry perspective there are good reasons for doing so. And it's happened before. In Alaska. With Exxon. A short history of how Prudhoe Bay came online is instructive for putting Point Thomson into context.

In 1968, ARCO, BP, and Exxon formed a pipeline consortium called TAPS (later renamed Alyeska), their shares of ownership proportional to that of the oil field itself. Because no single company controlled a majority share, every decision required negotiation and was the product of uneasy alliances between the rival companies. Furthermore, each company was in a position to thwart the others' plans whenever it saw a strategic advantage for doing so.

ARCO was a relatively small company at that time, certainly not struggling but not altogether stable either. It operated an extensive network of gas stations in the western U.S.—so-called downstream assets—but was lacking reliable sources of crude to feed into that market. Thus Prudhoe Bay was a life saver that guaranteed ARCO's economic health for decades. The company immediately began planning for a pipeline to Valdez. It wanted the oil now.

For its part, BP was also eager to push forward. The British company had long sought entry into the lucrative American retail market. It first acquired filling stations in the northeastern U.S. from Sinclair. A complicated merger with Sohio followed, in which BP's ownership share would decrease if production levels at Prudhoe Bay were not achieved by certain deadlines.

Clearly ARCO and BP had reason to move quickly and begin recouping their sizeable Alaska investments. Exxon was an entirely different story.

In those years the Texas-based company held worldwide crude reserves that could be developed more easily and cheaply than those at Prudhoe (still the case today). It simply didn't need Alaska crude as badly as did its TAPS partners. In fact, developing Prudhoe Bay quickly might have actually disadvantaged Exxon's global position by enabling the aggrandized ARCO and BP to introduce new oil into existing markets. When asked about his company's apparent reticence, Exxon chairman Mike Wright replied, "We aren't as eager as they."

In meetings of the TAPS Owners Committee, Exxon repeatedly voted against budget allocations for pipeline work.

In 1976, the State of Alaska commissioned Washington, DC attorney Terry Lenzner to study cost overruns on the pipeline. Officials believed that excessive and unnecessary expenditures could be withheld from calculation of the tariff, thus increasing revenue to the state. Lenzner's report documented Exxon's pattern of delay and found that it contributed to Alyeska's dysfunctional management structure, particularly in the consortium's early days when poor planning and inadequate budgets set the mold for a company prone to costly inefficiency.

Exxon may also have wished to avoid appearing overly committed to the pipeline so as to extract favorable concessions from the state. When faced with tax increases or environmental controls, for example, Exxon had no compunction about threatening to abandon Alaska altogether.

John Blair, an economist with the Federal Trade Commission, wrote of the industry's international machinations in the 1970s: "Confronted with a government action which they opposed, a few large owners would be in a position to keep the oil in the ground, secure in the knowledge that over a long-term inflationary period time would be on their side." Exxon could easily absorb any delay, even one lasting decades, if it kept alive some possibility of a better deal or more advantageous political position down the road.

Oil is a global game. History shows that even Prudhoe Bay, the largest oil field on the continent, is subject to the self-interested maneuverings of multinational industry players.

It should surprise no one that the much smaller Point Thomson isn't any different.

BIG STATE,
SMALL SCREEN

◆◆◆◆◆

Mike Gravel, as this column shows, pioneered the use of political TV ads in Alaska in 1968. Forty years later, he launched a largely forgettable presidential campaign notable for only one thing—its unique Internet ads. In one short clip Gravel stares silently into the camera for a full minute, then tosses a rock into a pond and walks away. The ads received over half a million hits on YouTube.

THE TRICKY THING about watershed historical moments is that they are often impossible to identify as they are happening.

After all, that's why we call it history. The legacy of current events can be fully assessed only with the remove of years—or even centuries. (There is a wonderful, if perhaps apocryphal, story about Zhou En-Lai, China's foreign minister under Mao Tse-Tung, who was asked about the influence of the French Revolution on western society and responded, "Too soon to tell.")

This is especially true in the world of politics where elections, by virtue of their immediacy, are notoriously poor indicators of historical significance. The "most important election in a generation" seems to come along every other year—even though very few actually are, and none in the moment.

Every now and then, however, a watershed event comes along whose impact is immediate and recognizable. The 1968 primary election was one such moment in Alaska politics: the emergence of television as a powerful campaign tool.

The primary featured two Democrats in the race for the U.S. Senate: incumbent Ernest Gruening and challenger Mike Gravel. The candidates' platforms were not that dissimilar, but their campaigns could hardly have been more different.

The 81-year old Gruening was a giant in Alaska politics with a public service resume that went back decades. As territorial governor and later senator, Gruening traveled extensively throughout Alaska, especially to rural villages, something no public official before him had ever done. Much of his political success was based on countless personal relationships forged at a time when the territory had a relatively small population. His was an era of old-fashioned, face-to-face politics.

After three decades in the public eye, everyone knew both his name and his record. You either liked him or you didn't. As a candidate for re-election in 1968, there seemed little for the senator to do but shake hands and say, "Hi, I'm Ernest Gruening." Which is pretty much what he did.

Mike Gravel, on the other hand, belonged to a new generation of politicians.

Gravel arrived in Alaska in 1956 with, as he later described it, a college degree and not much else. Following a stint with the Alaska Railroad, he embarked on a career in real estate and entered politics. With two terms in the State House under his belt, including one as speaker, Gravel decided in 1968 to challenge Gruening.

Gravel's first move was to retain Joe Napolitan, a Washington, DC pollster and political consultant. Although commonplace today, campaign handlers like Napolitan were a rare breed in 1968, especially in the political hinterlands of Alaska. His hiring by the Gravel campaign foretold a media-savvy professionalism never before seen in the North.

Ernest Gruening and Mike Gravel MIKE GRAVEL COLLECTION, BOX 843, FOLDER 14, ALASKA AND POLAR REGIONS, RASMUSON LIBRARY, UNIVERSITY OF ALASKA FAIRBANKS

Polls conducted by Napolitan showed Gravel trailing, but within striking distance of Gruening. The pollster rightly concluded that most everyone had their minds made up about the incumbent. Gruening's numbers were stagnant and there seemed little he could do to boost his popularity. In response to polling data that showed Gruening's age as his number one liability, Napolitan advised the 38-year old Gravel to emphasize his youth and energy.

Alaska's population, always young and transient, had more than doubled in the last two decades. The newcomers wanted jobs, roads, and economic development of every kind. While Gruening distributed a stuffy campaign biography that lauded his past accomplishments—ancient history to the newcomers—Gravel published a series of essays under the title *Jobs and More Jobs*.

Gruening also suffered for his outspoken stance against the Vietnam War. A more careful politician might have toned down his rhetoric, but the loquacious Gruening was never one to hold his tongue or turn down a high-profile speaking engagement. Although Gravel shared the incumbent's opposition to the war, he also recognized the hawkish view of most Alaskans and kept his thoughts to himself. When asked directly about Vietnam, Gravel gave vague, generic answers. It was yet another example of the professional politician working every possible angle.

Gravel's masterstroke, however, was a 30-minute film entitled *A Man for Alaska* that played up his humble beginnings, military record, and business acumen as a successful real estate developer. The film aired multiple times on every TV station in Alaska in the two weeks before the primary. It showed seventeen times in Anchorage alone. Gravel staffers took the film to rural villages (where TV did not yet exist) and held screenings with free popcorn.

Campaign films were nothing new. Gruening himself had made one in 1962. But what set Gravel's apart was its poll-driven message, professional production, and market saturation. The film proved the decisive factor in the race. Gravel, who trailed in nearly every poll throughout the campaign, pulled ahead in the final week as his film dominated the airwaves. He won the primary and went on to defeat Elmer Rasmuson in the general election.

The Gruening-Gravel primary ushered in a new era in Alaska politics where candidates were polished and packaged for TV. Future candidates would follow Gravel's example, running TV spots that emphasized style on par with substance. The young state had quickly caught up to the nationwide trend. The ubiquity of televised political ads in Alaska had begun.

a
CENTURY
of
POLITICAL
MELODRAMA

•••••

One measure of James Wickersham's standing in Alaska is the number of natural landforms named for him. There are six—a mountain, two creeks, two domes, and a cliff on the west face of Mount McKinley that he attempted to scale in 1903. Add to that his homes in Juneau and Fairbanks, both of which remain open as museums, and the many streets and buildings named in his honor, and it becomes clear the legacy of Wickersham is quite literally stamped all across Alaska.

What more can be said about the year 2008 that will surely go down as one of the most incredible in the history of Alaska politics? Ted loses his seat, Don keeps his. And then there's Sarah. (If you're looking for historical precedent for a shake-up of this magnitude, the closest you might come is a five-month window in 1968-69, when Governor Wally Hickel left Juneau to become Nixon's Interior Secretary and both U.S. Senate seats changed hands—Ernest Gruening lost his seat to Mike Gravel, and Bob Bartlett died while in office and was replaced by Ted Stevens.)

In lieu of spilling even more ink on the 2008 election, let's take a look back exactly one hundred years at another political melodrama that had lasting consequences for Alaska: the election of James Wickersham to Congress. His rise to power included elements that are still a feature of

James Wickersham JAMES WICKERSHAM-1, ALASKA
STATE LIBRARY

campaigns today—political shenanigans, media bias, sex scandals, and the
supposed noble struggle of the common people against special interests.

In early 1908, James Wickersham was a very happy man. The former
federal judge had resigned from the bench to open his own law practice
in Fairbanks. He earned more money in his first month as lawyer-for-hire
than he did in an entire year as judge. Wickersham was also relieved to
be free of the political backbiting that made his years on the bench such
an ordeal. Opponents in Congress consistently blocked his official confirmation, forcing the judge to serve by a series of recess appointments.
He now relished his newfound freedom as a private citizen.

Before long, however, influential Republicans, including party boss
John McGinn, began pestering Wickersham to run for Congress (Alaska's
status as a federal district enabled it to send a non-voting delegate to
Washington). Wickersham refused, instead throwing his support behind
the incumbent, Thomas Cale. Following a series of nasty disputes and

James Wickersham's campaign headquarters in Nome. WICKERSHAM STATE HISTORIC SITES PHOTOGRAPH COLLECTION, P277-004-135, ALASKA STATE LIBRARY

near fistfights at the party conventions, Wickersham wrote in his diary, "Now I am glad I kept out of the delegate fight!"

By early summer, however, a vacuum appeared on the political scene.

Cale was nowhere in sight. He spent the summer on his family farm in Wisconsin, unsure about whether to run for re-election. A Republican splinter group nominated John Corson, a Seattle native whom Wickersham did not even consider a real Alaskan. And when little-known postmaster John Clum started attracting crowds, the calls intensified for Wickersham to step up and fill the void. Appeals to his vanity worked their magic on the reluctant lawyer. A steady parade of supporters marched into his office and begged him to save Alaska from the slate of unimpressive candidates. Assured of widespread support, Wickersham finally acquiesced.

On June 22, he declared his candidacy in the most dramatic fashion. He first enlisted his followers to infiltrate a Clum campaign event, then

"HIS MASTER'S VOICE."

A cartoon from the July 6, 1908, edition of the *Fairbanks Daily Times* depicting James Wickersham as a lapdog of the Guggenheim Syndicate. FAIRBANKS DAILY TIMES, 7/6/1908, P. 1

maneuvered to have supporter Ferdinand de Journal invited to speak. De Journal went down the list of declared candidates, expressing no strong feelings for any of them, and then declared that a "new man" was required for the job. When he named James Wickersham, the bombshell caused a spontaneous (not really) round of hoorays and foot stomping to erupt from the crowd. "The fat was out in the fire," Wickersham wrote. "I became a candidate!!"

Wickersham spent the following week visiting mining camps around Fairbanks. He hosted a "large and enthusiastic" meeting at Ester Creek where he was "heartily applauded." Despite these expressions of support from miners throughout the Interior, Wickersham withdrew from the race the following week. He had no money, no campaign organization, no newspaper endorsements, and, worst of all, came under heavy criticism for betraying his friend Thomas Cale—who still had not declared his intentions. "I am sorry that I made such a damned weak display of myself," he wrote in his diary. "I went up a little ways in a little balloon and forgot to take the parachute along."

Everyone knows politics is cyclical, however. Being down one day doesn't mean you won't be up the next. Wickersham received a telegram in mid-July: "Cale will withdraw if you will run." Just like that he was back in.

Wickersham approached the campaign with renewed vigor. To every newspaper in the territory he submitted his "declaration of principles," which included bread-and-butter issues like road construction and better mail service. Wickersham also called for some form of self-government (none dare call it statehood, not yet) to take back control of Alaska's resources from Outside corporations. He specifically named the Guggenheim Syndicate as the biggest plunderer. (If any of this sounds familiar, it's because Alaska politicians have been using these lines to electoral success ever since.)

Wickersham's platform received a welcome hearing with certain newspapers, namely W.F. Thompson's upstart *Tanana Miner*, while the more established dailies, the *Fairbanks Daily Times* and the *Fairbanks Evening News*, savaged him with the headlines "Gang of Wickersham Followers Starts a Riot" and "To Whom Did He Lie?" Political cartoons, including one with a crude caricature of Wickersham as a dog beholden to corporate masters, were a front-page staple of the *Times*.

The specter of a sex scandal even entered the race at one point. While addressing a crowd in Nome, Wickersham made a casual reference to living in his own house with his own wife—an offhanded remark that resulted in gales of laughter. Only later did he discover that a local politician was not-so-secretly cohabitating with a woman not his wife. Eager to avoid mention of his own moral failings (an extramarital affair years before had resulted in his arrest on charges of seduction) Wickersham engineered a truce with the embarrassed official.

Election Day found Wickersham on a steamer heading back to the Interior from Nome. Downed telegraph lines kept the ship's occupants unaware of the results for over a week. Wickersham arrived in Fairbanks to find confirmation of his victory. He garnered roughly 40 percent of the nearly ten thousand votes, easily outpacing the other four candidates.

The Delegate-elect claimed his win represented a triumph of clean politics over lies and corruption.

Wickersham would go on to serve seven terms as Alaska's delegate to Congress. He achieved passage of the Organic Act of 1912, which conferred territorial status to Alaska and created an elected territorial legislature. He also oversaw legislation creating the Alaska Railroad and the Alaska Agricultural College and School of Mines (now the University of Alaska). In 1916, he introduced the first Alaska statehood bill.

From that first election in 1908, which he twice had to be goaded into, until his death in 1939, James Wickersham established himself as the first great politician in Alaska's history.

REMEMBERING
a
GIANT

◆◆◆◆◆

Bob Bartlett never lost his sense of humor, even while being prepped for heart surgery at a Cleveland hospital in November 1968. As Claus-M. Naske wrote in his biography of the senior senator from Alaska, Bartlett asked the doctor to be especially careful because, in the event of the patient's death, "I have a strong feeling...the governor of Alaska would not appoint a successor of my political faith." Bartlett also insisted the doctor keep him alive another two years "so I may have the benefit and enjoyment that comes by reason of lower income taxes upon attainment of age 65." Unfortunately, Bartlett's poor health led to complications following the surgery and he died a few weeks later. (Indeed, Governor Walter Hickel appointed Ted Stevens, a Republican, to the Democrat's seat in the Senate.) This column was first printed in December 2008, four decades after the statesman's untimely death.

IT WAS FORTY years ago this month that Alaska lost one of its true giants. E.L. "Bob" Bartlett, the longtime territorial delegate to Congress and one of the state's first U.S. senators, died on December 11, 1968, following heart surgery. Although Bartlett considered his service in the Senate as the pinnacle of his career, in the long view of history it is his efforts on the statehood movement that stand as his legacy.

A Resident of Alaska for 39 Years—Fourth Division for Over 30 Years!

VOTE FOR

E. L. [Bob] Bartlett

Democratic Candidate for

Delegate to Congress

Primary Election, April 25, 1944
Endorsed by Delegate Dimond

90-176-323

Bartlett campaign advertisement from the 1944 congressional primary, his first run for public office. EDWARD LEWIS BARTLETT PAPERS, UAF-1990-176-323, ALASKA AND POLAR REGIONS, RASMUSON LIBRARY, UNIVERSITY OF ALASKA FAIRBANKS

Bartlett cut his political teeth in the 1930s as an aide to congressional delegate Anthony Dimond. The two men became close friends when Dimond, a lawyer from Valdez, began his rise from local to territorial to national office and Bartlett was a newspaper reporter on the politics beat. In 1939, President Franklin Roosevelt named Bartlett to the post of Secretary of Alaska. He moved his family to Juneau and began working with Governor Ernest Gruening, another FDR appointee. The two men would forge a working relationship (and often contentious friendship) that lasted decades and guided Alaska through some of the most significant developments in its history.

When Dimond decided not to seek re-election in 1944, Bartlett ran for his seat and won handily. As a non-voting delegate from a territory about which few congressmen ever gave a second thought, Bartlett sought to shepherd legislation through Congress the old-fashioned way: he made friends. Known for his relaxed demeanor and engaging conversation style, Bartlett simply charmed every other congressman and convinced them to support Alaska legislation on the basis of friendship. The Library of Congress estimates Bartlett passed more pieces of legislation than any other member in history.

On November 8, 1955, Bartlett addressed the Alaska Constitutional Convention in Fairbanks, devoting most of his speech to the issue of natural resources. Alaska would likely receive 100 million acres of land upon statehood, Bartlett told the delegates, and for the sake of future generations they had a responsibility to provide for its careful and equitable management:

> The taking of Alaska's mineral resources without leaving some reasonable return for the support of Alaska governmental services and the use of all the people of Alaska will mean a betrayal in the administration of the people's wealth.

Five decades later, Bartlett's words are as prophetic as they are stirring:

> Alaskans will not want, and above all else do not need, a resources policy which will prevent orderly development of the great treasures which will be theirs. But they will want, and demand, effective safeguards against the exploitation of the heritage by persons and corporations whose only aim is to skim the gravy and get out, leaving nothing that is permanent to the new state except, perhaps, a few scars in the earth which can never be healed.

Delegates to the convention took heed of Bartlett's warning and enshrined in the constitution the principle that Alaska's resources should be managed as a public trust for the long-term benefit of the people. The article on resources, like the constitution as a whole, is elegant in its simplicity. It does not mandate any specific code, but only sets the concept of public interest at the heart of all laws and regulations to follow.

No issue occupied Bartlett's attention more than statehood. Throughout his congressional career, he introduced numerous statehood bills and organized hearings in both Washington and Alaska. While other Alaska leaders swooped into the capital periodically to lobby Congress and garner headlines, Bartlett quietly and methodically spent years laying the groundwork for statehood, winning over one congressman at a time. When a statehood bill finally passed in 1958, more than one congressman attributed his 'aye' vote to a genuine personal affinity with Bartlett.

Bob Bartlett shaking hands outside the Baranof Hotel in Juneau.
EDWARD LEWIS BARTLETT PAPERS, UAF-1969-95-563, ALASKA AND POLAR
REGIONS, RASMUSON LIBRARY, UNIVERSITY OF ALASKA FAIRBANKS

For all his many friends in Washington, Bartlett was even more popular in Alaska. He never lost an election, often winning with a two-thirds majority and once garnering an astounding 81 percent of the vote.

On March 27, 1971, two and a half years after his death, a statue of Bartlett with the inscription, "Architect of Alaska Statehood," was dedicated in the National Statuary Hall of the U.S. Capitol. Lieutenant Governor Red Boucher stated, "His place in history is now inscribed in the halls of the nation's Capitol, the building in which he worked for fourteen long years to achieve statehood for Alaska."

A man without an antagonistic bone in his body and for whom politics was always a game of addition, never subtraction, Bob Bartlett deserves to be remembered as one of Alaska's great pioneers.

FIFTY YEARS
of
STATEHOOD:
THE HISTORICAL
PARADE

·····

The very first line of Alaska 50: Celebrating Alaska's 50th Anniversary of Statehood, *the glossy, quasi-official state publication on the matter, reads: "The name 'Alaska' comes from the Aleut word alaxsxaq, loosely meaning 'Great Land.'" Loosely, indeed. A more precise definition of the word is "main land," or more literally, "the object toward which the action of the sea is directed." Neither of these translations strikes the right tone of majesty, however, and so the editors of* Alaska 50 *simply changed it. This linguistic slight-of-hand is a prime example of how we embellish our stories to make them more inspiring. The story of statehood, as both* Alaska 50 *and this January 2009 column point out, is as changing as the Alaska weather.*

HISTORIANS LOVE ANNIVERSARIES. In January 2009, on the fiftieth anniversary of Alaska statehood, we were simply beside ourselves with nerdish glee.

The last few years have been a historical thrill ride, what with opportunities to commemorate the Constitutional Convention, the congressional vote on the statehood bill, and now Eisenhower's signature that made it official. And let's not forget that quite a few of the pioneers behind these events are still alive. These men and women are direct links to the

Alaska territorial governor Mike Stepovich (center) hand delivers the *Anchorage Daily Times* to President Dwight D. Eisenhower and Interior Secretary Fred Seaton following congressional passage of the Alaska statehood bill, July 1958. NATIONAL PARK SERVICE PHOTOGRAPH, DWIGHT D. EISENHOWER PRESIDENTIAL LIBRARY AND MUSEUM

past and their recollections have become a staple of every "fifty years of statehood" exercise in nostalgia.

It is worth noting, however, the difference between commemoration and historical analysis.

In a recent article in *Journal of American History*, Richard White notes that anniversaries are useful in linking the past and present, as well as a means for remaking both. The past is simultaneously remembered, forgotten, and remade in order to shape the present.

Think for a moment about every newspaper or magazine article you've read about the fiftieth anniversary of statehood. How many discussed it in terms anything less than glowing? How many treated the statehood pioneers, both living and deceased, as anything other than heroes? How many sang the praises of Prudhoe Bay, the Permanent Fund, and Ted Stevens—but contained not a word about the Alaskan Independence Party, the urban-rural divide, or any of the other messy issues that cannot be wrapped up with a pretty red bow?

That's the difference between history and commemoration. History is a book; commemoration is a parade. History deals with facts; commemoration celebrates a myth. History asks probing and sometimes uncomfortable questions about the past; commemoration forgets everything that doesn't honor the present. (Make no mistake, I am not anti-statehood nor do I think the event and its leaders are unworthy of praise. We simply must remember that celebrating a historical anniversary is not the same as studying our history.)

Examples abound with regard to Alaska statehood.

In the summer of 1958, the ink wasn't even dry on the statehood act before squabbling began over who should receive credit. C.W. Snedden, the right-leaning publisher of the *Fairbanks Daily News-Miner*, printed a series of editorials praising every Republican even tangentially connected to the movement, while pretending Democrats had nothing to do with it. He also called in a few favors in the publishing world to get Mike Stepovich, the Republican candidate for Senate (and heretofore lukewarm supporter of statehood), on the cover of *Time*.

Democrats also played the game, none better than Ernest Gruening who took to calling himself "Mr. Statehood," much to the dismay of his more modest and equally deserving colleagues. To read Gruening's memoirs is to be left with the impression that he achieved statehood all on his own. The names of his fellow leaders—Bob Bartlett, Bill Egan, Ralph Rivers, Bob Atwood, Fred Seaton, and others—appear infrequently and only as supporting players.

What Snedden and Gruening were doing, of course, was tearing down the history of statehood and rebuilding a myth that suited their present needs—all within fifteen minutes of the event itself! As William Faulkner famously put it, "The past is never dead. It's not even past."

The past was again deconstructed on the twenty-fifth anniversary of statehood in 1984, when a panel discussion featuring a mix of pioneers and historians took up the question of the *anti*-statehood movement of the 1950s. Panelists pretty much agreed that its arguments—the prospect of increased taxes and a jumble of bureaucratic regulations that would spell the end of the frontier spirit—more or less vanished the day the statehood act was signed. Yet even a casual glance at the political landscape today reveals those positions are still in circulation. They're no longer in the guise of opposing statehood (well, except for the Independence Party), but the anti-government, fiercely libertarian sentiment remains intact. Acknowledging both the existence and persistence of those views is not something you'll find in a statehood anniversary celebration, however.

Another example: following the passing in November 2002 of Peter Reader, a miner from Nome and delegate to the Constitutional Convention, state flags were lowered to half-staff and public officials noted with solemnity the passing of another Alaska pioneer. But—and no disrespect intended to Mr. Reader and his family—we must remember that Reader was the only convention delegate *opposed* to statehood. His participation in writing the constitution was minimal at best. In the entire three-month duration of the convention, Reader spoke aloud exactly once—a single sentence in which he expressed his enjoyment of the proceedings.

While it was certainly fine and proper to note Reader's passing, no one who saw the state flag at half-staff should have surmised that we'd lost a giant of the statehood movement. In many ways, lowering the flag was as much about commemorating the Constitutional Convention one more time as remembering the man himself.

The past does not belong solely to historians, as anyone who has attended a Fourth of July parade or Civil War reenactment can attest. Where commemorators are free to embellish the myth—adding or subtracting details to fit the narrative of the present day—historians are bound by rules. We may continually add to the analyses of the past, but never take away. Sometimes new or previously unexamined evidence affects our interpretations, though more often than not it is simply the passage of time and the layers of subsequent events that force us to reexamine the legacies of the past. What one historian wrote 50, 100, or 1,000

Alaskans proudly displaying a 49-star flag on January 3, 1959, the first day of statehood. From left: Ralph Rivers, Bob Atwood (holding flag), Interior Secretary Fred Seaton, Ernest Gruening, Bob Bartlett, Mike Stepovich, and Waino Hendrickson. ERNEST GRUENING PAPERS, UAF-1976-21-281, ALASKA AND POLAR REGIONS, RASMUSON LIBRARY, UNIVERSITY OF ALASKA FAIRBANKS

years ago is never really wrong. It's just that the world changed in the intervening years and made those histories obsolete.

That commemorators, politicians, filmmakers, and parade organizers remain free to remember, forget, and rebuild the story of Alaska statehood as often as is necessary doesn't mean historians can ever do the same. We can only attempt, from one anniversary to the next, to deepen our understanding.

TV
is
HERE!

⦁⦁⦁⦁⦁

When broadcasting pioneer Augie Hiebert first brought television to Anchorage on December 11, 1953, the inaugural program was "Sign On," a live 30-minute broadcast from the KTVA studio. The program featured a military band, choral group, and local singers and dancers. When Hiebert launched KTVF in Fairbanks fourteen months later the opening ceremony followed the same script. "It was an encore performance in every way," wrote Robin Ann Chlupach in Airwaves Over Alaska, *her biography of Hiebert. So Fairbanks's first TV broadcast was, for all intents and purposes, a rerun!*

THE TRANSITION FROM analog to digital TV begun in February 2009 and completed four months later was undertaken to free up broadcast space for public safety communications and allow for increased programming choices and improved picture and sound quality. In Alaska, a place that has traditionally lagged well behind the rest of the country in all things technological, the federally mandated switchover resulted in dumpsters filled with old TVs and suddenly obsolete rabbit-ear antennas. Let's take a look back at the very first TVs to arrive in Fairbanks.

The Northern Commercial Company displayed the first sets at the Tanana Valley Fair on August 20, 1953. A newspaper ad that same day proclaimed "TV IS HERE!" in bold letters. Hundreds of locals lined up for a peak at the future.

The sets ranged in price from $259 to $419 (an exorbitant sum in 1953 dollars) and featured a built-in antenna that provided excellent reception, according to local salesman Bob Wirth. He explained that only the shipping costs made TVs slightly more expensive in Alaska than in the rest of the country. Programming was still free thanks to national advertising. As if the TV alone wasn't amazing enough, Wirth further excited the masses with the prospect of programming on demand. A proposed joint venture with the phone company would allow customers who paid a subscription rate to order specific programs, such as Notre Dame football games.

But the benefits didn't stop there. "According to police records in the states," reported the *Fairbanks Daily News-Miner*, "a definite decline in juvenile delinquency has resulted when youth are thus entertained at home." (That the kids would also forsake exercise, eat prodigious quantities of chips and soda while on the couch, have their fragile minds corrupted by onscreen sex and violence, and get tendonitis in their thumbs from playing Grand Theft Auto 4 for nineteen straight hours—all that came later.)

For all the excitement that summer, the locals who went to the fair saw what amounted to nothing more than a lifeless box full of wires. There was no TV station in Alaska at the time. The Higgins and Rollins Company of Los Angeles promised that broadcasting would begin in Fairbanks on New Year's Day 1954, with five hours of programming each day.

In reality, it wasn't until February 17, 1955, that the Fairbanks airwaves crackled with picture and sound courtesy of KTVF and its founder Augie Hiebert. The broadcast began at 6:30 that evening with a 30-minute test pattern. One can imagine the thousands of hopeful eyes glued to screens all over town, no doubt the first and last time a simple test pattern was the highest rated program on TV!

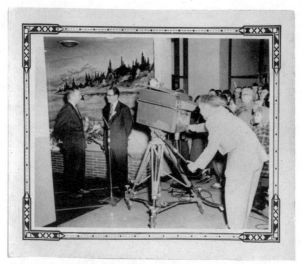

Broadcasting pioneer Augie Hiebert behind camera for "Sign On," a 30-minute live program on February 17, 1955, the first TV program in Fairbanks. ROBIN ANN HIEBERT

The KTVF Dedication Ceremony began at 7:00 p.m. sharp, broadcasting live from the lobby of the Northward building before a huge crowd of people who apparently didn't yet own TVs. The hour-long ceremony featured remarks by local dignitaries and performances by the Eielsonnaires (the airmen's choral group), Miss Liberty's hula dancers, and Mandrake the Magician. Network programming started at 8 o'clock with *The Life of Riley*, followed by *Going Places with Uncle George*.

"Downtown streets became literally deserted," reported the *News-Miner*, "as citizens crowded into bars and TV dealer showrooms to watch the proceedings."

This simple observation would prove prescient in defining the impact of television, not just in the Interior but on society as a whole. Its many benefits notwithstanding, this new form of entertainment irrevocably altered the social fabric of every community where it was introduced. In 1950, only 1 in 10 households in the U.S. had a television. By the end of the decade, 9 in 10 did. Almost overnight, television enabled people to remain indoors, avoid their neighbors, quit the bowling league, and so on.

This is no more evident than in Alaska's rural villages where television led to increased knowledge of national and world affairs, but also presented challenges to retaining traditional aspects of Native culture. Shortly after the arrival of satellite TV in Inuit villages throughout the Arctic, for example, one visiting journalist witnessed the virtual shutdown of communities at certain times of day. Entire families gathered around the TV in complete silence, their gaze riveted to daytime soap operas featuring blond, blue-eyed actors who spoke a language not everyone in the room even understood.

Numerous studies have shown that people who watch little or no TV are much more likely to volunteer in their communities, belong to civic organizations, or write a letter to their congressman. Those same people typically get more exercise and generally enjoy healthier relationships than those who watch several hours of TV each week.

Television isn't all bad, of course. Established by Congress in 1967, the Corporation for Public Broadcasting has a mandate to provide programs that engage often neglected audiences, especially minorities and children. Likewise, the development of rural programming in Alaska and northern Canada has enabled the wide dissemination of indigenous perspectives. For evidence of television's ability to connect and unite people, one can look to the JFK assassination, the moon landing, 9/11, or any of a hundred other historical events from the last sixty years.

Nevertheless, those who haven't yet purchased a new digital TV or a signal converter box may want to try going TV-free for a week or two. See how it goes. Take a walk outside instead of watching the tube. Write a letter to your mother. Bake a loaf of banana bread and bring it over to your neighbor. My guess is that after a couple of weeks you won't miss TV nearly as much as you thought you would.

ALASKA
or
BUST!

Anyone who doubts that newcomers to Alaska are often drawn by frontier idealism and notions of great adventure need only visit the Alaskana section of any used bookstore and peruse the self-published titles: Let's Go to Alaska, One Man's Homestead, Six Years of Alaskan Adventures, Why Would Grandma Move to Alaska?, Taming Mighty Alaska: An RV Odyssey, *and many, many others. This column, published in March 2009 on the fiftieth anniversary of the arrival of a group of Alaska Highway roadtrippers, describes how Alaskans themselves are occasionally caught up in the hoopla.*

As CLICHÉS GO, the station wagon with "Alaska or bust" painted on the door being driven north by some Midwesterner with more dreams than sense is probably the most tired of all. (I write this to disparage no one, for a decade and a half ago I was precisely such a down-states rube in a late-model sedan, though without any sign in the side window announcing my intended destination.)

The mother of all "Alaska or bust" stories happened in the spring of 1959 when twenty-one Detroit families set out on a 4,500-mile roadtrip with the intent of homesteading on the Kenai Peninsula. They called themselves the Detroit 59ers and for a few weeks in the spring of that year they captured the imagination of Michiganders and, somewhat surprisingly, Alaskans too.

The caravan, consisting of seventeen cars, six camper-trailers, and a large cargo van they named "The Monstrosity," assembled on March 5, 1959, in the parking lot of a drive-in theatre in west-central Detroit. The 59ers were mostly young, blue-collar families struggling in a stagnant Detroit economy where the unemployment rate had reached double digits. The prospect of free land in Alaska—homesteading claims could be obtained then for a filing fee of just a few dollars—convinced them to sell their homes and head north.

"We are pooling all we know how to do in this cooperative venture that probably none could do alone," said 59er spokesman Ronald Jacobowitz. The group included carpenters, machinists, mechanics, welders, bricklayers, and other tradesmen able to contribute to the communal nature of the endeavor. "Everything we are doing," said Jacobowitz, "every plan made and carried out has been done by the vote and consent of all."

The 59ers became instant celebrities in Detroit. Several hundred people turned out on the chilly morning the caravan left to cheer and wave good-bye, many thrusting gifts of food and money upon the grateful travelers. More than a few onlookers expressed admiration and even envy for the group's courage. *The Detroit News* assigned a reporter to travel with the group all the way to Alaska. *Life* magazine sent a photographer.

That the 59ers received so much attention back home is in no way surprising. The romance and mystery of the Alaska wilderness continues to launch a thousand trips north every year and elicits the wide-eyed admiration of those left behind (in a way moving to Des Moines never does).

Accordingly, the Detroit newspapers played up every Alaska stereotype during the course of the journey. "A cold expanse of snow and ice lies ahead," one paper reported. Alaska was surely a "wild country that will separate the men from the boys." The trip was "a gamble" and "a test of men against virgin soil." Snowshoes, log cabins, and grizzly bears all

Ray and Bernice Kula, two of the Detroit 59ers, in Edmonton, Alberta, beside the van they drove to Alaska. DETROIT NEWS

received prominent mention in news reports of the expedition. When nine families dropped out somewhere in Canada it spoke not of failure but confirmed the tremendous risk for the hardy souls that remained. What newspaper in Detroit wouldn't put that on the front page?

But if folks in the Lower 48 were awestruck by the whole affair, surely Alaskans remained immune to the hyperbole. No one here was going to be impressed, right?

Wrong.

"Anchorage Hosts 59ers Today" announced the headline of the *Anchorage Daily Times* on March 28. The state troopers escorted the caravan all the way from Palmer to a raucous celebration on Fourth Avenue that was crowded with well-wishers. The 59ers were feted in grand style with music, dancing, free mooseburgers, and speeches from local dignitaries. "It's great to be in Alaska," remarked Jacobowitz.

Why the red-carpet reception? Aren't sourdoughs supposed to look down their noses at cheechakos?

The timing of the 59ers could not have been more perfect. They arrived in Alaska just a few months after statehood when the air buzzed with the promise of economic prosperity. Any pioneer with an axe, a shovel, and a dream to open the country was welcome. "We need people," stated Senator Ernest Gruening. Anchorage mayor Hewitt Lounsbury chimed in, "You are the first pioneers of the new state." Many compared the 59ers to the Matanuska Colony, a New Deal program that brought hundreds of families from the upper Midwest to Alaska in the 1930s.

Bob Atwood, editor and publisher of the *Anchorage Daily Times*, had long supported any and every form of development in Alaska. He was fond of saying he hoped to see the state achieve a population of one million someday. "Success of these people is important to every Alaskan," he wrote in an editorial welcoming the newcomers. "They are symbolic of the thousands of others who want to come here and make a home."

Other Alaskans cut through the rhetoric, however, and struck a more cautious tone. Merrill Weir, head of the Alaska Employment Bureau, sent releases to newspapers in the Lower 48 advising prospective emigrants to stay home. Unemployment in Alaska was pushing 20 percent, according to Weir, and only a few skilled professions, such as dentistry and court reporting, were lacking for applicants. Senator Bob Bartlett, his office deluged with requests for information about homesteading opportunities, replied to every letter with a warning about the years of backbreaking work required to clear a homestead.

The 59ers encountered such hardships quickly after settling in Alaska. Most returned to Michigan after the first summer. A few toughed it out for a couple of years before heading back south. Of the twenty-one families that originally started out from Detroit, only four successfully obtained a homestead patent by clearing, improving, and living on the land for five years.

"Growing up there was one of the best things that ever happened to me," Nicholas Rubino told the *Detroit News* four decades later. "Everyone pitched in to help each other build their houses. If your car broke down, you used someone else's. It was like being part of one big family."

Bill Orzechowski, another 59er who never gave up, lived in a small Quonset on his homestead near Trapper Creek. "My heart is in Alaska," he responded when asked why he toughed it out all those years. Orzechowski, the last of the 59ers in Alaska, died on March 6, 1984—one day after the 25th anniversary of his departure from Detroit in the "Alaska or bust" caravan.

a
SCREAMING
COMES
ACROSS
the
SKY

•••••

This column takes its title from the famous opening lines of Gravity's Rainbow by Thomas Pynchon: "A screaming comes across the sky. It has happened before, but there is nothing to compare it to now." (Similarly, no comparison is intended between any part of this book and Pynchon's masterpiece!) Where Gravity's Rainbow refers to Germany's V-2 rockets piercing the skies of London during the Second World War, the column here tells the story of a different rocket and how it—almost—lit up the skies of Alaska.

HAD YOU BEEN standing outdoors in Tok, Alaska, on the afternoon of Monday, December 29, 2008, you would have heard a tremendous explosion from above and a low rumbling that continued for several seconds. Looking up you would have seen squiggly contrails streaking across the clear sky. Had you picked up the phone and called the State Troopers, you may very well have been placed on hold, as dozens of other Tok residents were calling at that same moment to report the strange occurrence.

Although the most likely explanation was a crashing meteor, those who witnessed the event speculated on all manner of possibilities—secret military operations, a plane crash, or perhaps even a visit by aliens from outer space.

As you might expect in a place as big as Alaska, this wasn't the first time a mystery object exploded in the sky. One of the more curious incidents occurred just outside Delta Junction on November 30, 1957, and concerned a man-made satellite called Sputnik I—or so it seemed at the time.

Launched by the Soviet Union on October 4, 1957, Sputnik was first observed in this country by University of Alaska scientists as it passed over Fairbanks in the middle of the night. "A bright star-like object moving in a slow, graceful curve across the sky," is how C. Gordon Little of the Geophysical Institute described it. For several weeks both the satellite itself and its rocket booster, from which it had detached upon reaching space, continued to circle the Earth. Scientists around the world tracked the orbits for both objects and by the end of November determined that while Sputnik's trajectory remained fairly stable, the rocket was likely to reenter the atmosphere very soon. In fact, it could fall at any moment. It was due to make its final pass over Alaska on Saturday, November 30, at 3:37 p.m.

That afternoon at about twenty past three, a hunter named Victor Carrado was getting into his jeep near the Big Gerstle River outside Delta Junction when he saw a huge fireball shooting across the sky. According to news reports of the incident, Carrado instinctively ducked as it flew over his head and crashed into a distant grove of trees. "I thought it was going to hit me," he told officers at Fort Greely where he drove to report what he'd seen.

Archie Olmstead, a truck driver for the Big Delta Fuel Company, also reported a fiery object flying in a southwesterly direction. Gene Rogge of Fairbanks saw the object from his house at 11th and Gillam. It was about three feet in size, he stated, flying at a terrific speed with a hundred-foot flame trailing behind. A carpenter named Paul Spriggs, his wife, and their two young daughters had just returned home from doing volunteer work at their church in Delta Junction when they saw something flash across the sky and explode a moment later. The incident frightened the girls, Spriggs stated.

Researchers from the Geophysical Institute track Sputnik I at the Ballaine Lake tracking station in October 1957. GI director C. Gordon Little is fourth from left with his back to the camera. GEOPHYSICAL INSTITUTE, UNIVERSITY OF ALASKA FAIRBANKS

Another person who observed the fireball that afternoon was Dr. Little, the deputy director of the Geophysical Institute who eight weeks earlier had been one of the first to witness Sputnik and was now staring at the sky hoping for a glimpse of the rocket. The fiery object appeared in roughly the right location and at approximately the correct time, so he initially believed that's just what he'd seen. As dozens of eyewitness reports came in over the next three hours, however, Little realized the timing was off. The fireball had been observed a full sixteen minutes earlier than the rocket's calculated flyover time—a significant margin of error considering one complete orbit around the globe took only ninety-six minutes. Little also realized the reported trajectory of the fireball did not match the rocket's flight path.

That evening he telephoned Fred L. Whipple, head of the Smithsonian Astrophysical Institute, who asked how long the object had been visible in the sky. Upon hearing the flight lasted just five seconds, Whipple agreed it could not have been the rocket but was most likely a meteor. The much heavier rocket would have flown at a slower speed than a tiny meteor and left an entirely different flame trail.

Soldiers from Fort Greely searched the area by ground and air for the next two days, but found no trace of either rocket or meteor. A subsequent snowfall blanketed the area in white and convinced the Army to call off the search.

The actual fall of the Sputnik rocket probably occurred within hours of the Alaska incident, though the exact time and location are unknown. The last confirmed observation in North America was made by a radar station in California, which proved the rocket was still airborne when the mystery object crashed near Delta Junction. The Soviets charged that pieces of the rocket did indeed fall in Alaska and that the Americans refused to give them back. In response, the U.S. Naval Research Laboratory released orbit projections showing the rocket probably landed in Soviet-controlled Mongolia. Sputnik the satellite burned up while reentering the atmosphere on January 4, 1958.

But the question remains: What were the chances of a meteor coming down in Alaska within minutes of the rocket's expected final pass overhead? Dr. Little, no doubt relying less on scientific certainty and more on plain intuition, set the odds at one in a million.

BOOKS,
TOBACCO,
and
CIVILIZATION

•••••

> *"The rascality of Alaska has flocked here," wrote Hudson Stuck about Fairbanks in the early 1900s. "The whole of Front Street is given over to saloons." The comment, according to historian Tom Alton, goes a long way to explaining the missionary's efforts to open a library that would cater to the population's more intellectual qualities. The plan must have worked because the new library, according to Alton, made over 10,000 book loans in its first year of operation, including 1,106 to the town's children.*

HUDSON STUCK, THE Episcopal archdeacon of Alaska and the Yukon, gave a public lecture in Philadelphia in late 1908. One of those in attendance was a banker and philanthropist named George C. Thomas. While flipping through a picture book, he chanced upon a photograph of a few rough-and-tumble working men perusing a collection of books and magazines. They were gold miners seated in the reading room of St. Matthews Mission in Fairbanks, Alaska.

The gold rushes of the North held a particular fascination for Thomas. While he had never visited Alaska and had no plans to go, he greatly admired the hardy men and women who challenged the frontier. Thomas asked Stuck about the photograph and learned the miners in Fairbanks were eager for intellectual nourishment.

Three years earlier, when the booming town on the Chena River boasted a population of 5,000, with thousands more in the surrounding gold fields, a group of miners met with the Reverend Peter Trimble Rowe in hopes of acquiring what they called "mental food." In response, the bishop opened a small room in St. Matthews and filled it with newspapers and magazines donated by Episcopal parishes across the nation. The mission quickly had enough reading material to begin a mail-by-request service for the villages.

Hearing this, Thomas seized upon the idea of providing the town with a proper library. He donated $4,000 for the construction of an "unpretentious structure," and pledged another $1,000 yearly for three years for its upkeep. Thomas attached only one stipulation to his gift—the library had to double as a smoking room so the men could enjoy their tobacco while reading.

Archdeacon Stuck brought Thomas's vision back to Fairbanks where city leaders put up additional funds to expand the library's size and design. In spring 1909, construction began on a square, log structure with large windows on each side and a sloping roof that covered wide galleries on the north and east sides of the building. The library featured dual reading rooms—the promised smoking alcove and a second space for family learning and recreation.

Named for its principal benefactor who had passed away just as construction began, the George C. Thomas Memorial Library opened with a dedication ceremony on August 5, 1909. Archdeacon Stuck, who had donated the first books to the new library, spoke fondly of Thomas and his desire to bring knowledge and civilization to the frontier. The people of the Interior should be proud to have such a fine library, he told the overflow crowd at the dedication, and must now pitch in to take proper care of it. James Wickersham, Alaska's delegate to Congress, agreed: "Nearly everyone has a book or so that he can spare. Let him donate that to the good of the cause and for the glory of enlightenment."

George C. Thomas Library in Fairbanks CURTIS R. SMITH PHOTOGRAPHS, CA. 1917, UAF-1997-59-14, ALASKA AND POLAR REGIONS, RASMUSON LIBRARY, UNIVERSITY OF ALASKA FAIRBANKS

In July 1915, the Thomas Library hosted the historic meeting between the Tanana chiefs and U.S. government officials, including Wickersham. The chiefs, numerous elders, an interpreter, and an Episcopal missionary represented the Athabaskans of the Interior in discussions on native land claims, work opportunities, and education. In rejecting a government proposal to establish reservations, the chiefs launched what would become a decades-long struggle for recognition of their cultural and aboriginal rights to the land. The effort culminated in the Alaska Native Claims Settlement Act passed by Congress in 1971. For its historic value as the site of the first meeting, the library was listed on the National Register of Historic Places in 1972.

The Episcopal church sold the building to the city in 1940 for exactly one dollar on the condition that it always be used as a library. The promise lagged after 1977, when the books were moved to the new Noel Wien Library and the building was leased as a commercial property. The building's current owner, John Reeves, has announced plans for a mining library.

Like Mr. Thomas a century ago, the people of Ester have turned their bookish ambitions to action by establishing the John Trigg Ester Library. In fact, it's pretty much a repeat of history. There are more books than available space and plans for a new building on Village Road continue apace (there will not be a smoking room this time around, however). And while the George C. Thomas Memorial Library was dedicated to "the divine uses of enlightened civilization," the extent to which the John Trigg Library accomplishes the same feat in Ester remains to be seen.

it's
FAIR TIME!

✦✦✦✦✦

When a group of Seattle businessmen decided to host an Alaska-Yukon-Pacific Exposition in 1909, the plan infuriated Alaskans who felt it was just another example of outsiders profiting at their expense. In a 1991 article in Alaska History, *Terrence Cole pointed out that most believed simple greed was behind the effort. Cole quoted W.F. Thompson, publisher of the* Fairbanks Daily News-Miner, *who wrote: "If there is a dollar of Alaska money…not being worked for Seattle's benefit, Seattle wants to know it, and to change that condition." Another newspaperman (and future territorial governor), J.F.A. Strong, noted: "Seattle has grown like Jack's beanstalk upon the outpouring of Alaska's natural wealth, and the industry of the territory's hardy and adventurous citizens, and now she wants to trade upon the Alaskan name. She plans a mighty exposition for her own profit [and] labels it the Alaska-Yukon-Pacific Exposition which is somewhat like stealing the livery of heaven to serve the devil in." It surely came as no surprise to Thompson, Strong, and other Alaskans that the Exposition did indeed put Seattle's economic interests first.*

To say that Alaska is economically tied to Seattle is an understatement of the highest order. Our freight is shipped through Seattle. Most of our domestic flights are routed through Seattle. Alaska Airlines itself is based there. Throughout its history, much of Alaska's harvested resources—gold, salmon, timber, coal, oil—have made their way to market via Seattle. Flip through the Seattle Yellow Pages and you will find dozens of companies with "Alaska" in their names, everything from insurance firms to seafood processors to art galleries.

This economic link goes back to the very founding of the two respective locales, but was made manifest a century ago with the opening of the Alaska-Yukon-Pacific Exposition. A world's fair in everything but name, the AYP Exposition opened on the University of Washington campus on June 1, 1909, and promised to showcase the wonders of the North. Those with monetary value, at least.

Seattle's business community unabashedly promoted the exposition "to exploit the resources of Alaska and the Yukon" and establish their city as the center of the region's commercial development (take that, Portland and San Francisco!). Organizers noted over seven million people lived within a radius of one thousand miles of Seattle, and that opportunities for trade and capital investment appeared everywhere you looked. In recognizing the importance of foreign imports/exports, the exposition added the Pacific to its theme and invited Japan to participate.

When people at the turn of the century thought about Alaska, gold was likely the first thing to come to mind. Accordingly, the exposition's Alaska Hall displayed an impressive array of gold bars and nuggets worth $1.25 million (securely locked within a huge iron cage, no touching allowed). The Arctic Brotherhood, a fraternal organization with chapters in most gold mining districts in Alaska and the Yukon, hosted visitors in what the newspapers called "a novel log building for a meeting place." The exposition further played up Arctic stereotypes with an Eskimo Village that featured indigenous peoples from Labrador, Alaska, and Siberia, as well as faux glaciers, dog teams, and igloo-style dwellings made of caribou hide. A statue of William H. Seward, the man who engineered the purchase of Alaska in 1867, rounded out the display.

And that, one might say, was pretty much that.

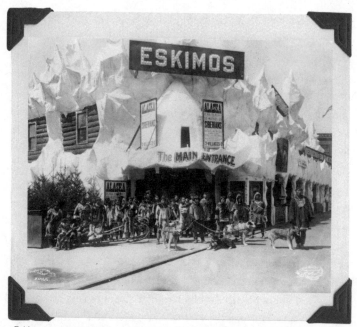

Eskimos and a sled dog team standing in front of the Eskimo Village at the Alaska-Yukon-Pacific Exposition in Seattle in 1909. FRANK H. NOWELL ALASKA YUKON PACIFIC EXPOSITION PHOTOGRAPHS, NA 2215, SPECIAL COLLECTIONS DIVISION, UNIVERSITY OF WASHINGTON LIBRARIES

For a fair with the words "Alaska" and "Yukon" in its very title, the Seattle-based exposition offered a surprisingly cursory view of the North in favor of promoting economic growth right there at home. The State of Washington sponsored dozens of exhibits in its Forestry Building, Fisheries Building, Agriculture Building, and Good Roads Building. King County had its own building, as did the states of Oregon, California, Idaho, and Utah. Canada was there. Hawaii and the Philippines too. Even New York State had a building!

The extent to which the AYP Exposition misplaced its northern focus at times bordered on the absurd. Visitors could observe reenactments of Civil War battles, and the official AYP postcard book included images of

Custer's Last Stand, stage coaches in Yellowstone Park, and the Arizona desert. The book contained exactly one photograph from Alaska (Front Street in Nome) and none of the Yukon.

But all of that is neither here nor there when you consider the whole point of a fair is to get paying customers moving through the turnstiles—and boy did they. The exposition attracted 80,000 people on opening day alone. By the close of the fair four months later, 3.7 million people had toured the grounds. Not only was the AYP Exposition a runaway financial success, it more than doubled the number of buildings at the University of Washington (a handful of which are still in use today) and transformed the campus from a sleepy outpost in the woods to a landscaped center of community activity.

And the exposition's impact on Alaska? Hard to say. The dream of Seattle's business elite to "exploit the resources of Alaska and the Yukon" certainly came true in the ensuing decades—although those developments likely would have occurred with or without the fair's faux glaciers and fur-clad Eskimos. Nonetheless, the AYP Exposition permanently cemented the economic relationship between Seattle and Alaska, for better or worse.

FROM
THEIR
COLD
DEAD
HANDS

•••••

With the obvious exception of the National Rifle Association, the gun rights movement in Alaska is something of an ad hoc affair. Petitions are circulated and letters turn up in the newspapers from time to time, but the actions are usually not the result of a planned campaign but rather the work of individuals who are momentarily inspired. The Fairbanks chapter of the Second Amendment Task Force might seem like a more coordinated effort, but for all the heat and light accompanying its founding in February 2009, the group is largely the work of one man who, consciously or not, drew upon decades of Alaska history for his pro-gun platform.

IT MIGHT OTHERWISE have been just another Monday night in February at the "Farthest North Denny's in the World," except that a young man named Schaeffer Cox has a thing about firearms and decided to call a meeting of what he named the Second Amendment Task Force. One hundred and twenty people showed up—and it wasn't for the Denver omelets.

"Let it be known," reads a letter unanimously approved by the assembled gun owners that night, "that should our government seek to further tax, restrict or register firearms or otherwise impose on the right that shall not be infringed…that the duty of us good and faithful people will not be to obey."

The SATF warned that gun control leaves law-abiding citizens unable to defend their person and property. The passage of even a single law, according to the group, opens the floodgates to more regulation and before you know it there's a federal agent knocking at your door in the middle of the night.

The founding of a gun rights group in Alaska is as natural a political act as you'll find. That Cox's group, relying mostly on word-of-mouth advertising, drew ever-increasing numbers to its meetings, culminating in a "Freedom Fest" held at the Carlson Center, suggests nothing particularly extraordinary beyond the fact that many in Alaska love guns and need little encouragement to sign the roster of any group dedicated to preserving that right.

In fact, a short history of pro-gun activism in Alaska shows that Cox and the SATF are treading a well-worn path.

In January 1947, U.S. Marshal Stanley Nichols induced the territorial legislature to consider a public safety bill requiring the registration of all pistols and revolvers. Just days later, in the face of no organized opposition, the Fairbanks Chamber of Commerce endorsed the proposal. Guess what happened next.

The Tanana Valley Sportsmen's Association sponsored a radio program on KFAR and placed full-page ads in the local papers. "No pistol-control law has ever been enacted which had any determinable effect in reducing armed criminal activity," the TVSA stated. The group further noted that any such law, no matter how limited in scope, would be the first step down a very slippery slope, at the bottom of which lay tyranny. TVSA President Arthur Hayr compared those in favor of gun control to Nazis and Communists. The legislature killed the bill barely a week later.

Fast forward two decades to the summer of 1968. In the wake of the assassinations of Martin Luther King, Jr. and Robert Kennedy, Congress considered various gun control measures, including a nationwide registration system, ownership bans for certain classes of individuals (i.e., convicted felons and the mentally ill), and prohibitions on the transport of firearms across state lines. Letters of protest appeared almost daily in

Four boys with toy pistols in Point Hope, Alaska, c. 1953. MARY COX PHOTOGRAPHS, 1953-1958, UAF-2001-129-136, ALASKA AND POLAR REGIONS, RASMUSON LIBRARY, UNIVERSITY OF ALASKA FAIRBANKS

Alaskan newspapers, nearly all of them featuring the same vocabulary of the 1947 fight.

"These proposals," wrote Daniel B. Hawkins of College, "would in no way prevent further assassinations but would serve ultimately to prevent the law-abiding citizen from owning firearms of any kind." Rudy Voigt of Fairbanks agreed: "To register guns creates a hardship on hunters and sportsmen and is only the first step to taking our guns away." It was the slippery slope argument all over again (one that apparently failed to resonate with Congress as it would ultimately pass the Gun Control Act of 1968).

A movement at that same time to voluntarily turn in unwanted guns to police achieved some traction in parts of the U.S., but the State Troopers reported not a single firearm was surrendered in Alaska. "Wouldn't that be something," wrote a clearly agitated Lynn S. Langfield of Fairbanks, "for all honest people to turn their guns in, so there would be no protection against crime anywhere in the nation." Here was another trope from the earlier gun rights movements in Alaska—gun laws only harass and disarm regular folks, leaving society vulnerable to criminals unafraid to wield unregistered firearms.

Those dirty Reds also made a return appearance. "If the Communists did attempt to take over," wrote Elmer Brisbols of Anchorage, "the registration records of all guns [would] fall into the hands of the wrong people."

From a historical perspective, it's fascinating to see how the language remains the same. The arguments are interchangeable from one era to the next. One can see the same phenomenon with nearly every interest group. Environmentalists, for example, have been recycling the language of Thoreau, Emerson, and Muir in defense of wilderness for more than a century.

To further illustrate the point, let's take a little quiz. Read the three quotes below, all penned by Alaska gun owners, and see if you can guess which was written in 1947, which in 1965, and which in 2009:

A. Our forefathers fought and died to establish the rights of individual action and liberty . . . . Let us not render these sacrifices, which have been so willingly placed on the altar of freedom, futile by permitting internal aggression on the liberties and rights of honest citizens.

B. In these last years we have taken some giant strides on the road to socialism . . . . America, the land of the free and the brave, is going down the drain and so-called Americans are hastening to assist the dissolution.

C. To the extent that our government violates [the Constitution] it nullifies its own authority, at which point it is our right and duty, not as subjects but as sovereign Americans, to entrust this power to new stewards who will not depart from the laws we have given them.

You can't tell, can you? And that's precisely the point. In the universe occupied by gun owners, the barbarians are always at the gate, America is always under attack from within, and the example of our revolutionary forebears is the only one that can save us. (Answers to the quiz appear at the end of this column.)

So where does this leave Schaeffer Cox and his followers? The present challenge for the Second Amendment Task Force, which Cox describes as more of a movement than a group (which then begs the question why it's called a "task force," but I digress), is how to sustain momentum for a cause with no clear challenge to its central mission. Reports of fatal shootings somewhere in this country turn up in the news every week, but almost none result in a renewed call for stricter gun laws. And once you set aside all rhetoric about "eternal vigilance in the face of threats unseen," there is little reason to think any public official in Alaska seriously entertains the notion of gun control. Even Mark Begich, the first Alaska Democrat elected to Congress in a generation and favorite "liberal" target of local conservatives, boasts an A rating from the National Rifle Association.

Whatever course of action the SATF ultimately takes, history shows that the language used to articulate both its pro-gun platform and the nature of the impending infringement on their rights will be identical to that of past campaigns. Case in point: The answers to the quiz above are A = 1947, B = 1965, and C = 2009. But then it hardly matters, does it?

SEWARD
in
ALASKA

27

◆◆◆◆◆

That William H. Seward gave a public address in Sitka, Alaska, on August 12, 1869, is beyond dispute. His exact words are harder to pin down. The text printed a week later in The Alaska Times, *then the territory's only newspaper, contained spelling errors that suggest it was the product of a harried stenographer. A version printed in national newspapers and pamphlet form the following month was significantly longer, more rhetorically sophisticated, and almost certainly drafted by Seward after he departed Alaska. The audience for his "Sitka address," as the speech came to be known, was not Sitkans—it was the eastern political establishment with whom Seward hoped to quash the "Seward's Folly" business once and for all. As a historical record the revised speech, whether actually delivered or not, accurately represents Seward's thoughts on Alaska at the time and is the one on which this column is based.*

EVERYONE KNOWS THE 1867 purchase of Alaska was engineered by William Seward, secretary of state to presidents Lincoln and Johnson. Much less remembered is the fact that Seward himself visited Alaska two years later for a firsthand look at his procurement, what would come to be recognized as one of his singular accomplishments as a public official.

In August 1869, Seward traveled by ship through the Prince of Wales archipelago, up Peril and Chatham straits, Lynn Canal, and as far north as the Chilkat River and Fairweather Glacier, where he marveled at the "eternal snows" of Mount St. Elias in the distance. During a brief sojourn at Sitka on his return south, Seward was asked by the locals to give a public lecture. He acquiesced with an address that began, "It is altogether natural on your part to say, 'You have looked upon Alaska, what do you think of it?' Unhappily I have seen too little of Alaska to answer the question satisfactorily." Despite this earnest confession, Seward went on to explicate with remarkable precision Alaska's present condition and what he saw as her future challenges.

"Alaska has been as yet but imperfectly explored," stated Seward. "But enough is known to assure us that it possesses treasures of what are called the baser ores equal to those of any other region of the continent." He then listed copper, iron, coal, and gold—all in such abundance and value as to guarantee their future harvesting. Timber, too. And the resources of the sea, according to Seward, would continue to provide opportunities for commerce just as they had for the Russians for more than a century.

If his knowledge of the region's resource potential seems prescient, keep in mind that Alaska was not such an unknown quantity at that time as the "Seward's Folly" wisecrack might suggest. Americans knew there was more than icebergs and polar bears up there. New England whalers and the Hudson's Bay Company had been established fixtures of the regional economy for decades. In a speech supporting the treaty of cession, Senator Charles Sumner of Massachusetts similarly made mention of Alaska's well-known bounty: "quintals of fish, sands of gold, choicest fur, [and] most beautiful ivory."

Matters of politics and government found mention in Seward's Sitka speech. At a time when mocking "Walrussia" comics still appeared in newspapers, Seward was already talking statehood: "Within the period of my own recollection, I have seen twenty new States added to the American Union, and I now see, besides Alaska, ten Territories in a forward condition of preparation for entering into the same great po-

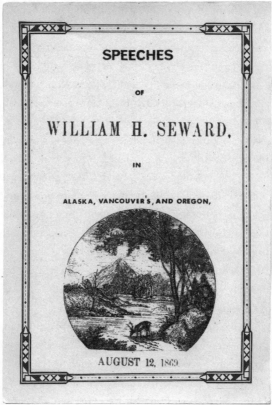

Pamphlet of William Seward's 1869 speeches in Alaska and the Pacific Northwest. SPEECHES OF WILLIAM H. SEWARD IN ALASKA, VANCOUVER, AND OREGON, AUGUST 12, 1869

litical family." Forty-three years before Alaska achieved territorial status and ninety before statehood, Seward said this: "The political society to be constituted here, first as a Territory, and ultimately as a State or many States, will prove a worthy constituency of the Republic." (Seward knew his speech would be printed in newspapers back east, and if there was a self-validating quality to his optimism it may have been directed at his many critics.)

With the theme of American expansionism now hanging in the air, Seward addressed the presence of a foreign territory situated between the U.S. and Alaska: "British Columbia, by whomever possessed, must be governed in conformity with the interests of her people and of society upon the American continent." It was no great secret that Seward hoped to annex the Canadian territory, nor that many of its residents were not altogether opposed to the idea. But Seward, ever the diplomat, addressed the topic with caution and tact a couple weeks later in a speech in Victoria: "The loyalty of British subjects here is fully acknowledged and respected on my part. . . . On the other hand, I freely confess that it is my political ambition to see the United States of America transcend even the British nation in civil and religious liberty, and usefulness to the human race." Seward left open the question of actual governance, thus there was enough in his Victoria speech to placate everyone. Canadian loyalists heard that he would leave them alone; U.S. sympathizers heard that American liberty was on the way. (British Columbia became a Canadian province two years later.)

Seward's mention of Alaska's indigenous peoples bears many hallmarks of the paternalistic attitudes common of the day. The words *uncivilized*, *savage*, and *warlike* are repeated throughout this section of the speech. "Oppression and cruelty occur even more frequently among barbarians than among civilized men," stated Seward. But he lamented how the absence of confederation between Native nations foretold a political and cultural decay, especially in the face of the superior power called the U.S. Government: "It is manifest that, under these circumstances, they [Alaska Natives] must steadily decline in numbers, and unhappily this decline is accelerated by their borrowing ruinous vices from the white man." It would be another three or four generations before indigenous peoples banded together into an effective political force, while "ruinous vices" (i.e., alcohol, drugs, and sugary snacks) continue to decimate Native communities.

At the time of Seward's visit to Alaska, the first great gold strike was still a decade in the future, the first oil well three decades away, and the establishment of a territorial government barely on the horizon. Nonetheless, Seward foresaw how the history of Alaska would unfold:

> *Emigrants go to every infant State and Territory in obedience to the great natural law that obliges needy men to seek subsistence, and invites adventurous men to seek fortune where it is most easily obtained, and this is always in the new and uncultivated regions. . . . Emigrants from our own States, from Europe, and from Asia, will not be slow in finding out that fortunes are to be gained by pursuing here the occupations which have so successfully sustained races of untutored men.*

As a general description of Alaska, this one is spot on.

the
LINE
in the
SNOW

University of California professor Hayden White has long expressed the view that historical narratives are not unlike works of fiction. Both utilize textual constructions of people, places, and events—plot, in other words—which in turn are the products of a writer's literary talents. Because even the most objective historian has to make endless subjective decisions in crafting a narrative (i.e., word choice and ordering of events) the result can justifiably be called a "story." But what happens when a writer explicitly tries to do both? How do we respond to a book that by design contains elements of historical fact and invented fiction? Read on...

ONE OF THE newest and most thought-provoking books on Alaska history is not a work of history at all. It's a novel.

The Snowflake Rebellion, by Anchorage writer Tom Brennan, belongs to the genre of historical fiction where invented characters act out made-up storylines against the backdrop of an actual historical era. Colin Callihan, the novel's taciturn hero, is an oil industry geologist who achieves professional success (he single-handedly discovers a huge deposit of North Slope crude), personal failure (his wife leaves him for an environmentalist and he falls into the booze), and is eventually reborn as the leader of an Alaskan secessionist movement (he carries a gun and people call him Commander).

Although the timelines are rather fluid, the book's historical setting is more or less Alaska's modern oil age, from the mid-1960s to the present day. The author uses Prudhoe Bay, the pipeline, and every other milestone of that era to drive the narrative. People, too. Wally Hickel, Arliss Sturgulewski, Joe Hazelwood, and many others—even Emmitt Peters, the champion musher from Ruby—all make appearances, or rather their thinly-disguised Doppelgängers from this alternate universe do. (Don Young is called Dick Davison in the book and serves in the Senate, not the House, but he still clamps wolf traps on his arm when necessary to make a point.)

But what really makes the book so interesting—and I don't necessarily mean that as a compliment—is how Brennan conflates fact with fiction in such a way that his Alaska is enough in focus to be recognizable, but fuzzy to the point of being unfamiliar.

Joe Wechsler, the character modeled after Alaskan Independence Party founder Joe Vogler, meets his demise not at the hands of a drifter over a botched robbery (which is what happened to Vogler in 1993), but in a shootout with federal agents trying to evict him from his homestead. For the general reader this version makes for a more enthralling tale and, as a plot device, propels the secessionist movement even closer to the rebellion of the book's title. As a historian, however, I wonder about the suitability of having characters do things their real-life antecedents never actually did.

Let me make a rather crude analogy. Take the movie *Titanic*, another blend of fact and fiction. Leonardo DiCaprio and Kate Winslet can meet, fall in love, do whatever they want—as long as at some point the ship hits the iceberg and sinks. But what if the filmmakers changed the historical narrative? Sent the ship down from a fire in the engine room, for example, or a freak tidal wave? Or even worse, suppose they didn't sink the ocean-liner at all but had it arrive in New York to great fanfare! Moviegoers would ask for their money back.

That's an extreme example, but to a lesser degree that's just what Brennan is doing in *The Snowflake Rebellion*. Consider, for example, the novel's unnamed oil tanker that runs aground and disgorges its cargo of crude into Prince William Sound. In Brennan's fictional telling, the industry had a fleet of planes ready to deploy and attack the crude with dispersants that would have minimized the ecological damage. But environmentalists, who had previously agreed to the tactic, pulled a double-cross and hampered the response with their obstructionist ways. While the industry clean-up teams stood by and waited, the greenies and their political lapdogs in Washington dithered and the slick eventually got out of control.

Well, that's one way of setting the scene. And to be fair, since Brennan's book is a work of fiction he can write anything he wants. But had he decided to track the historical record of the *Exxon Valdez* just a little more closely he would have noted the use of dispersants was problematic for a number of reasons, not least of which that nobody really knew how to use them. Or, for that matter, that the terminal's entire cache of response equipment, booms and the like, lay under several feet of snow. Or finally that the industry had no idea what it was doing and utterly failed in its long-standing promise to protect the environment.

Although the genre of historical fiction comes with an implicit license to dramatize certain events, one has to consider whether we want our stories to be more historical or more fiction. Michael Chabon's *The Yiddish Policemen's Union*, an award-winning novel that imagines Sitka as a settlement for Jewish refugees during the Second World War, has the same sort of casual relationship with the truth—yet Chabon takes as his point of departure an event that never happened and wonders if it had. Brennan, on the other hand, takes actual events from the past and rewrites them. Where is the line, and how do we know when an author has crossed it?

Because certain real-life events in Brennan's book are described so accurately, those areas where the author deviates from the historical record cannot be accidents, but must be conscious acts of revisionism, a deliberate reframing of acknowledged facts. Ascertaining authorial intent is always a tricky proposition, but it's probably no great stretch to say that Brennan writes this way to validate his worldview (as he did for years as an editorial writer for the pro-development *Anchorage Times*). Take a Google-assisted tour of Brennan's old columns and you'll find there isn't a problem facing Alaska that can't be traced back to East Coast liberals or the National Park Service.

Now that I'm 900 words into this column, it may be too late to state my intent is not to critique Mr. Brennan's book; rather, I mean to raise the larger question of how we *use* history (or abuse it, as it were).

What we call "history" has undergone a fragmentation, especially over the last few decades, where the outmoded idea of historical truth has given way to multiple interpretations, often from the heretofore marginalized points of view of women, minorities, the poor, etc. No longer the exclusive domain of white Protestant males, History (with a capital 'H') now belongs to everyone. Old stories are being told in new ways, and new stories are being told for the first time. It's not just kings and queens and the rise and fall of empires, but everyday people and ordinary events. Our understanding of the past now requires a complete integration of these varied perspectives. I should mention this is generally a good thing.

The trick, of course, is that when everyone owns history, no one does. All too often we're left without a coherent narrative of our collective past. We rely instead on convenient facts and selective interpretations. We create stories, not histories. Where we once consulted encyclopedias and almanacs, hefty tomes written by professionals you reasonably assumed filled every page with truth, we now have Wikipedia, a pinnacle of open access knowledge that is really just an ambitious work of historical fiction written by thousands of authors less concerned with conveying information than in simply telling stories they know to be true, which are then edited by other authors who think they know more—which, come to think of it, is pretty much what those encyclopedia and almanac writers did, too. Whither the truth?

Reenter Mr. Brennan. His novel is certainly not bound by the rules of historical analysis, but that doesn't make it any less of an attempt to "own" that which he describes. (He was there. He saw what happened. He *knows*.) Indeed, poets and storytellers have been doing that very thing for millennia. In a sense, Brennan is doing nothing with Alaska history that Homer didn't do with the Trojan War, or Shakespeare with Henry V at Agincourt, or even Mel Gibson in the movie Braveheart—the film's many historical errors aside, how many people would even know the name William Wallace were it not for that 1995 Oscar winner?

Though I would never endorse *The Snowflake Rebellion* as history—nor would I even call it a good read; it's really quite awful—I acknowledge its ability to challenge assumptions about how history should be told.

the
ALASKAN
CITY

◆◆◆◆◆

For readers of this book who have never been to Fairbanks the
mention below of the Johansen Expressway will mean nothing. Yet
if you've ever been to a Home Depot or a Wal-Mart, or driven down
a billboard-cluttered highway in any mid-sized city in America,
one that features absurdly placed stoplights and incomprehensible
frontage roads—you'll get the gist. Even a highway commercial
district of the type described in this chapter has within its layout
some sort of historical continuity. We built it. It came from some-
where. How our cities develop from the moment of their founding
says a lot about who we are. I was inspired to write this two-part
series after reading the essays of John Brinckerhoff Jackson, a keen
observer of American cities who was capable of appreciating and
bemoaning them simultaneously—which is how many of us feel
about parts of urban Alaska.

I. JACKSON'S LAMENT

THE WORST SIN of the box store mishmash on the east end of the
Johansen Expressway is not its ill-conceived layout and labyrinthine traffic
pattern, nor its crass commercialism, nor the way these national chains
are hurting local retailers—although those sins by themselves are certainly enough—no, the primary transgression is that it marks, once and
for all, our disconnect from the natural world.

Cities need not be soulless. Even when comprised of steel, concrete, and glass, with nary a tree in sight, urban areas can still exhibit a certain harmony with natural forms. A shopping mall, for instance, if designed with arched doorways and a sunlit atrium can represent a welcoming social landscape. But the Home Depot-WalMart-Lowe's aggregate? It requires that we be automatons, that we learn the maze of frontage roads and navigate accordingly. And for what reason would we do otherwise? There are no pleasant distractions, nothing to stop and look at. The signs direct us from one parking lot to the next. The streets all lead somewhere; none are destinations themselves. It is a most unwelcoming environment.

If only we'd listened to John Brinckerhoff Jackson. Until his death in 1996, Jackson was this country's leading voice on the potential richness of human-centered geography. In 1951 he founded a journal called *Landscape*, which acquired a small but devoted following of architects, planners, engineers, and others with an interest in the ways people leave their marks on their surroundings. Brinck, as he was known to his many friends, had little patience for the then-bourgeoning environmental movement and what he saw as its singular, misplaced concern with untouched wilderness. He vastly preferred what a neighborhood laundromat could tell of the human condition.

He was not a myopic urbanist, however. For Jackson, the city was a place where relationships developed not only between people, but between humans and the forces of nature. He viewed the city as a human-nature symbiosis, two dissimilar organisms coexisting for the mutual benefit of each. Just as animals build nests, dens, lodges, and other habitable small-scale environments—all the while utilizing natural forms and their inherent efficiencies—so there is nothing unnatural about humans doing the same. The crime, according to Jackson, occurs when we disengage from the natural world, when we forget that moving a pile of earth alters both the physical and mental landscapes we inhabit.

Local farmers don't make that mistake. They successfully manage human-created environments along nature-oriented principles (industrial mega-farms are another matter entirely). But the lessons of the rural landscapes never seem to translate to the urban ones. Jackson's lament, in other words, concerns our stubborn tendency to create jumbles of buildings and mazes of roads that occasionally satisfy our physical needs but never our psychological ones:

> We know that every time we heap up a mass of masonry or cut through a hill or drain a swamp or plant a row of trees or fill the air with smoke or pave an open area we are to some extent changing the local climate, the local environment, and changing our own physical condition. It is merely a question of putting this local knowledge to intelligent use in the design of cities. . . . [I]t is puzzling to note how little the average urbanist seems to care about the climate he is unwittingly creating, or about how it can be controlled.

It wasn't always this way. Consider the familiar grid pattern found in almost every town in the U.S.—blocks with uniform lots framed by streets at right angles to one another. Because of its organic simplicity the design can hardly be said to have an inventor. But Thomas Jefferson, who abhorred cities and had few good things to say about them, nonetheless wrote approvingly of the urban grid as a means for producing what he called "virtuous citizens." For all its tedium and predictability, the grid actually represents an egalitarian ideal of sorts where townspeople are encouraged to be citizens (as opposed to simply residents), active in the democratic process by virtue of their shared circumstance.

Take Fairbanks, for example. From its founding in 1902, the city developed organically along this Jeffersonian ideal. First Avenue fronted the river, with Second in parallel behind, then Third, and so on. City leaders even brought civic order to the red-light district by sequestering all vice and carnality to a Fourth Avenue hidden behind tall wooden fences. Following the May 1906 fire that destroyed much of the city and all of downtown, citizens petitioned for zoning ordinances that would create alleys, setbacks, and other firebreaks. While little about the city's

145

Aerial view of Fairbanks, circa 1923, showing the Jeffersonian grid that evolved from the Chena River outward. JOHN URBAN COLLECTION ANCHORAGE MUSEUM, B64.1.491

design could be considered natural—if we take the term to mean "of nature"—this degree of planning, such as it was, conforms to Jackson's concept of a local environment that encourages social relationships in their most elemental state. In this sense, a city block functions no differently than an ant colony, beehive, or coral reef, with its inhabitants achieving both personal and communal interests simultaneously. It is the perfect human-nature symbiosis.

The Fairbanks grid provided boundaries that facilitated the development of political, economic, and social institutions. The concept also applies to the thousands of miners up in the hills. In staking their claims they brought order to the landscape—not with an artificial geometric grid, but along the natural contours of the land, rivers, and creeks. The miners' tribunal, for example, was a self-administered judicial system whose authority derived from the egalitarian use of the land.

To cite another example, in present-day Ester the layout of the fire station, park, post office, and village square represents not only the center of the community's social environment—i.e., where people meet and do stuff—but also the landscape where they are encouraged to actively contribute to the health of the community.

All of which brings us back to the East Johansen. From the arrival of the Interior's first automobile in 1908 to the opening of Home Depot in 2002 and right up to the present day, we have created landscapes that continually fracture human-nature relationships in favor of speed and individual convenience. We transformed downtown streets into a series of one-way hamster tunnels that facilitate movement and discourage just plain looking around; we built Airport Way, with its hideous concrete barriers and chainlink fences; and we allowed the McDonald's on Geist Road to erect golden arches high enough to be seen by hungry students on campus, not to mention astronauts. The Johansen itself is nothing but a means for getting from one side of town to the other as quickly as possible. A more unnatural design is hardly conceivable.

But wait.

Pile Driver Roadhouse

UNDER NEW MANAGEMENT

Accommodations for 35 People.

Private Rooms for Ladies.

Excellent Dining Room Service.

Can Stable 48 Head of Horses.

Hot and Cold Water in Stables.

Warm Building for Campers.

Rates $4.00 per Day

H. A. HADLEY & JOHN MORGAN
Props.

Newspaper advertisement for the Pile Driver Roadhouse. Note the list of amenities, including "private rooms for ladies," designed to entice travelers on the Richardson Trail. WALTER T. PHILLIPS, ROADHOUSES OF THE RICHARDSON HIGHWAY, VOLUME II, ALASKA HISTORICAL COMMISSION STUDIES IN HISTORY NO. 172

Never beholden to the hobgoblins of foolish consistency, landscape scholar J.B. Jackson actually saw great beauty in such strip malls, diners, highways, parking lots, and the like. To him, they were valid expressions of human creativity as worthy of admiration as any more "natural" urban environment. In the next section I will take a second, more appreciative look at the East Johansen using this alternative view.

II. JACKSON'S APPRECIATION

J.B. Jackson would have found the profusion of big-box stores on the East Johansen endlessly fascinating. For Jackson, the American highway was a perfectly egalitarian social environment where motorists of every station engaged one another in a common dialogue. The desire to be in motion was what brought them together. The motels, drive-ins, gas stations, and other commercial enterprises that sprang up to support the endeavor represented an extension of that creative impulse. Yes, Jackson saw urban blight—but he also spied possibilities for American beauty:

> The highway has its many shortcomings, aesthetic, economic, and social; it is often ugly, inefficient, and destructive to many communities. Yet even the most cluttered, the most garish and vulgar specimen has an immense potential. . . . It often seems that America is evolving a taste for a new kind of beauty: cleancut geometric forms, primary colors, vast smooth surfaces and wide spaces uninterrupted by any detail, and bright lights. It is the beauty of newness, efficiency, and cleanliness.

Jackson wrote the above passage in 1966, more than three decades before the opening of Home Depot in Fairbanks, yet his words are an apt description of the best the East Johansen can offer. No one can say shopping at those box stores isn't comfortable, nor that the smooth facades and bright colors of the buildings themselves aren't welcoming in their own way. The exhibitionist architecture of roadside establishments is part of the dialogue of the highway. In such a transient landscape, those signs and structures that shout the loudest are heard. The strip is a social environment like no other.

The very first land route to the Interior, the Valdez-Fairbanks Trail, likewise functioned as both transportation corridor and social construct. Started at the turn of the last century by the Alaska Road Commission (led by Wilds Richardson for whom the highway would later be named), the Valdez-Fairbanks Trail began as a bushwhacked path passable only in winter. Roadhouses opened along the trail, the distance between them roughly that which a sled dog team could cover in a day. These were utilitarian, no-frills establishments where travelers got a warm fire, a hot meal, and a bunk that may or may not have qualified as comfortable. Some of the early roadhouses were just canvas tents. The true appeal, of course, was the social contact to be had after the isolation of the trail. The route came to be identified by its roadhouses—Yost's, Tenderfoot, Pile Driver, and many others—whose names alone promised warmth and became the "mental map" that guided travelers.

As the trail improved over the years, eventually allowing automobile travel, the roadhouses found themselves competing for travelers' patronage. Suddenly a lumpy cot and bowl of leftover stew just wasn't enough. Some proprietors attempted a touch of class by using the word "hotel" and advertising "accommodations for ladies." Others put up signs that boasted of spring mattresses, fresh vegetables (even in winter), indoor stables for horses and dogs, and other amenities. The dialogue of the trail was changing. Though certainly different from the neon signs and burger joints of Jackson's highway, the Valdez-Fairbanks Trail similarly transcended functionality and became part of the social landscape of its time.

Ask anyone who has driven the 414-mile haul road from Fairbanks up to Deadhorse and they'll speak of the excitement you feel the closer you get to Coldfoot, the only full-service hotel/diner/gas station for the road's entire length. Even the hypothetical driver with plenty of gas, a cooler full of food, and a thermos of hot coffee—in short, the one with no particular need to stop—will nonetheless pull over at Coldfoot. The desire to speak to another human being, or even just wander through the store for the distraction it offers, is too appealing to resist. As Jackson put it: "The best of all landscapes, the best of all roads, are those which foster movement toward a desirable social goal."

The proposed road out to Nome, an idea that has been kicked around more or less since the town's founding in 1900, also fits this theme. Though its purpose is ostensibly clear—so that Nomeites can drive out and everybody else can drive in—the appeal lies more deeply in the Jacksonian tradition of highways as social constructs. Every boomer with a Ford F350 longs for the road less because he actually needs or wants to go to Nome (*getting there* has never really been the hot-rodder's point), but that such a route would be yet another tableau on which to express speed and motion. The dialogue of the road beckons more than the road itself. The 24-hour truckstop sure to spring up in Ruby or Galena or someplace else along the highway would be popular not just for the blueberry pie and the pretty waitress on whom every trucker has a secret crush, but for the same reason the roadhouses of the Valdez-Fairbanks Trail thrived. They were not merely establishments along the route—they *became* the route.

And again we're back to the East Johansen, a social environment defined by the draw of its attractions. Is it garish? Yes. A thriving social landscape? Absolutely. The unfortunate result of nonexistent city planning? Yes, that too. Are we slightly ashamed by our expedient impulses as we check prices at Lowe's or eat burgers at Chili's? Is the strip beautiful, sterile, comfortable, inefficient, exciting, and repugnant all at the same time—in other words, is the East Johansen your typical American highway?

J.B. Jackson called these *vernacular landscapes* in that they reflect how people actually live. We choose this common language for its simplicity and convenience. To say that Jackson found such highways fascinating, however, does not necessarily mean he was enamored of them. Of their ephemeral nature he wrote: "A landscape catering to our gregarious instincts is certainly better than one which isolates us; but are we not capable of something more productive and permanent?" That, I would argue, remains an open question here in Alaska. The appeal of the open road is often its very lack of tradition which allows for any manner of behavior, language, and dress—qualities that also refer to Alaska in general. We are not constrained by tradition. We are free to act as we choose. We speak in the vernacular. But let the enduring nature of constructed roadside environments show that we will always, in ways large and small, be bound by history.

MONUMENTAL
ALASKA

◆◆◆◆◆

Charles Bunnell had every intention of leaving Alaska for good in August 1921, when the Board of Trustees of the soon-to-open Alaska Agricultural College and School of Mines (now the University of Alaska Fairbanks) offered him the job of president. He accepted, only to have his political foe James Wickersham maneuver to have the offer rescinded. The college was Wickersham's baby. He had achieved passage of the enabling legislation in Congress and the wily Republican recoiled at the thought of a Democrat like Bunnell being placed in charge. A motion to oust the president failed, however. Had he turned down the job and left Alaska as planned, or had Wickersham's gambit succeeded, Charles Bunnell never would have led the college for nearly three decades and today there would be no statue of him in the center of campus. I was inspired to write this column one day when I saw several students dashing past the statue and wondered how many of them knew its identity. Furthermore, do they realize what monuments are even for?

THERE IS A statue of a man on the University of Alaska Fairbanks campus that probably one in a hundred students could identify. Of that number, only one in a dozen could likely tell you anything more than the man's name—who he was and why there's a statue of him in the first place.

The bronze likeness of Charles Bunnell, first president of what was then the Alaska Agricultural College and School of Mines, is a monument of a largely outmoded style that honors a single individual for his accomplishments. As such, the memorial reminds us of something important—Bunnell's university—and places upon every professor and student the obligation to continue that legacy. "I have him in the graduation robes," said sculptor Joan Bugbee Jackson. "It not only signifies his office as president of the university, but hopefully, that's what the students of the university are there for." Standing there in his academic regalia, Bunnell implores us to continue his life's work and not let him down.

The same is true of other monuments to individuals. The Washington Monument and Lincoln and Jefferson memorials, for example, do more than just honor the men—they simultaneously remind us to care for their bestowals of freedom and democracy with great devotion. They are monuments as social contracts.

There is another type of monument, however, one of a more generalized nature.

Following Lincoln's speech at Gettysburg, a call arose to dedicate the entire battlefield as a memorial to those who fought and perished there. By the same token, many war memorials, especially in small towns across the country, are not in praise of generals or commanders, but rather obelisks, arches, or statues of an anonymous young soldier. The contract is the same, but exists independently of temporal personages and fleeting memories.

This may help to explain why so few UAF students today are aware of Charles Bunnell and his inestimable contribution to the institution where they are presently enrolled. Contemporaries die or move away, memories fade, and after a time every personal connection with the honored man is lost. There is quite simply no one left to remember. The obligation to continue Bunnell's work diminishes in direct proportion to how quickly we forget the identity of the statue.

Statue of Charles Bunnell, first president of the University of Alaska. GALEN LOTT

The same fate befalls the monument to George Parks, the man for whom the highway connecting Fairbanks and Anchorage is named (technically it meets up with the Glenn Highway forty miles outside of Anchorage, but the distinction is commonly ignored). No one recalls that Parks was a former territorial governor. If thought is ever given to the subject at all it is likely the mistaken assumption the Parks Highway is so named because it abuts Denali. The monument to Parks, a simple plaque at a roadside pullout seven miles outside of Ester, is unmemorable. Vandals have painted graffiti on the large stone to which it is affixed, and from the condition of the plaque itself it appears someone once took a few swings at it with a hammer.

Of the second type of monument, one dedicated to a certain event or group, a representative example is the Unknown First Family statue in downtown Fairbanks. Clad in winter clothing and huddled together in both unity and warmth, the anonymous figures represent millennia of human habitation in Alaska's Interior. The monument carries no names or dates, and thus suggests a more colloquial relationship with the past. It recalls an open history in which everyone had a role, as opposed to that limited to kings, presidents, and generals.

Another example is the Lend-Lease WWII monument, also on the river in downtown Fairbanks. Two unidentified airmen, one American and one Russian, stand together in the fight against fascism. Their gaze, as is nearly always the case with these types of monuments, is uplifted and cast toward the far horizon. As we begin to see history less in terms of named heroes and more as the product of contributions made by everyday people, the monuments we erect reflect that judgment.

Just outside the Trans-Alaska Pipeline terminal in Valdez stands a statue of five laborers who are representative of the tens of thousands that built the pipeline. The monument not only gets points for diversity (the Teamster is a woman, another is Alaska Native), but similarly recalls a glorious past owned by everyone who punched the Alyeska timeclock. They could have commissioned a statue of Alyeska president E.L. Patton or chief engineer Frank Moolin, the two men most responsible for constructing the pipeline, but the effect would have diminished over time. But the anonymous five workers? You don't have to know who they are to appreciate what they stand for.

It is this type of colloquial monument currently in vogue. A recent memorial in honor of the Alaska Territorial Guard, a WWII defense force comprised primarily of Alaska Natives, naturally features a statue of an anonymous young soldier in a parka, rifle in hand.

Dedicating a statue of a specific person today seems a rather pretentious notion, no matter the suitability of the claim. (Can anyone envision a groundswell of support for a statue of, say, Jay Hammond? Wally Hickel?) We eagerly name bridges and airports for men and women of distinction— but recalling the *good old days* requires an open monument in which everyone can see their reflection. Names and dates become irrelevant; all that matters is the historical continuity between this generation and every previous one. The past then belongs to us all.

LET'S PAY
as
LITTLE
as
POSSIBLE

•••••

Some years before becoming Alaska's governor, Ernest Gruening attended a cocktail party in New York where a mining executive boasted that he had the Alaska legislature in his pocket and therefore paid no taxes on his businesses there. "He had rooms in the Gastineau Hotel [in Juneau] and would dispense whiskey freely to the legislators; it was as easy as that to secure their grateful compliance," Gruening wrote in his memoir. The executive really should have kept his mouth shut, as Gruening would make the overhaul of Alaska's tax regime his primary focus as governor.

IN LATE 2009, when Lieutenant Governor Craig Campbell formally announced his candidacy in the next year's election, he called himself a budget hawk and told reporters, "I want to make sure Alaska residents never have to pay an income tax, or statewide sales tax, to receive the services that government is obligated to provide to the residents."

Setting aside the chronologically ambitious nature of the lite gov's remark—"never" is a long time for a political promise, certainly longer than his term in office not to mention his time on Earth—it was still a pretty good way to launch a campaign. Nobody in Alaska likes taxes, and Campbell's strident stance was sure to appeal to a broad constituency.

The taxman in Campbell's rendering, however, is pretty much a straw man. Alaskans haven't paid a state income tax since 1980, and no one is seriously talking about reinstituting one now. We have an entire generation of young voters for whom the very idea of a state tax on income is beyond their personal experience. For that matter, how many Alaskans of every age even remember the state income tax—how it came to be in the first place and why we got rid of it? More importantly, what effect does this brand of historical amnesia have on our ability to conduct an earnest public debate about our civic and fiscal obligations?

When soon-to-be governor Ernest Gruening first visited Alaska in 1936, he found a territory whose fiscal house was in appalling disarray. There was no uniform tax code for businesses, no property tax outside incorporated towns, occupational license fees that made little sense, and a corporate tax structure so feeble that natural resources worth millions were harvested by Outside companies with minimal return to residents. Worse still, Alaskans didn't seem to mind. The territorial legislature consistently squashed any talk of tax reform. Some towns refused to incorporate so as to avoid having to pay for their own basic services. "The towns here have precisely the same attitudes toward the territory as the territory has toward the federal government," an exasperated Gruening wrote. "Let's pay as little as possible and let the territory and federal government do it all."

Upon assuming the governorship in 1939, Gruening made overhaul of the tax code his highest priority. His allies warned it would be a tough fight. Gruening proposed a modest revenue system that included taxes on property, corporate income, and personal income—the last aimed squarely at the territory's many seasonal workers (e.g., fishermen and construction workers) who until now took every penny of their earnings out of Alaska. Gruening also made reference to the burgeoning statehood movement, noting that Congress would be disinclined to admit Alaska to the union so long as its residents insisted on having the federal government pay for everything.

Ernest Gruening being sworn in as Alaska's territorial governor in 1939 ERNEST
GRUENING PAPERS, UAF-1976-21-55145, ALASKA AND POLAR REGIONS, RASMUSON
LIBRARY, UNIVERSITY OF ALASKA FAIRBANKS

It is a testament to Gruening's determination that he stood behind
his plan for a full decade (an absolute epoch in political time) before it
was finally passed by the legislature in 1949. By that time, the territory
had debts of $3 million with mere thousands in the general fund. There
was no money to pay teachers. Private citizens were signing bank notes
to obtain loans for public projects. Alaskans came to realize it was time
to pay their own way.

Gruening made many enemies along the way, of course. No public
official can ever institute new taxes without being reviled by a select few.
Yet history has shown the tax measures were one of Gruening's most important accomplishments as governor. The tax policy put Alaska on a more
solid economic footing and paved the way for greater self-government.

Jay Hammond JAY HAMMOND COLLECTION, UAF-1984-200-
1, ALASKA AND POLAR REGIONS, RASMUSON LIBRARY,
UNIVERSITY OF ALASKA FAIRBANKS

Fast forward thirty years to the late 1970s. Oil is flowing down the pipeline and the state is awash in cash. Citizens are miffed at having to pitch their own pennies into the pot when the state had more oil revenue than it knew how to spend. An initiative to repeal the state income tax easily garnered enough signatures to make it on the ballot. Before that could occur, however, the state legislature convened a special session in September 1980, and voted nearly unanimously to not only repeal the tax but do so retroactively to 1978, so that every taxpaying Alaskan received a fat refund check. It's probably no coincidence this all happened six weeks before the election.

Although he ultimately signed the bill, Governor Jay Hammond opposed a total repeal from the start. "If we abolish the income tax," he told the Fairbanks Chamber of Commerce in 1979, "we will further reduce the direct personal stake that is created when people help pay for their own government." Hammond instead advocated an annual dividend from the Permanent Fund that would help offset the tax burden for residents, while leaving non-residents and seasonal employees subject to the full tax on income. When that proposal foundered the governor next suggested a ten-year moratorium on income taxes that would end just about the time oil revenues were set to peak and start their inevitable decline.

In the end, of course, the legislature found a complete repeal too tempting to resist. During the late 1980s and early 1990s—the very timeframe when Hammond correctly predicted state spending would begin to outpace falling oil revenues—a number of proposals to reinstitute the income tax surfaced but went nowhere.

In many ways, we find ourselves today in the same position we were in back in 1936, when Ernest Gruening recognized that Alaskans had gotten used to the free ride. Not paying taxes had become a habit and budget shortfalls were lamented but never really fixed. Winning people over required a tectonic shift in public sentiment that took ten years and a brush with bankruptcy to accomplish.

Today, after three decades of no income tax and twenty-eight PFD checks (and counting), Alaskans have grown so accustomed to the present fiscal state that a similar shift will be necessary to even start the discussion. But campaign pabulum of the type offered by Lt. Gov. Campbell—"never an income tax"—suggests it will once again be an uphill fight.

the
MYTH
of
ALASKAN
EXCEPTIONALISM

•••••

There is a persistent idea that Alaska is somehow "exceptional" in comparison to the rest of the country, that the "Last Frontier" has forged a unique regional character and pioneer spirit that are extinct everywhere else. Historian Roxanne Willis writes the image is "perpetuated in popular literature, wildlife documentaries, and political cartoons, as well as in the ubiquitous urban myths about the region." The average American believes Alaska is the land of polar bears, pristine wilderness, and brutally cold winters, whereas the reality is that fast food, strip malls, and cable TV are more representative of most Alaskans' daily lives. This "strange collection of cultural misunderstandings," as Willis calls it, sustains both outsiders' views of Alaska and Alaskans' views of themselves. Whether the image is accurate hardly matters. That's how myths work, after all.

A FEW OF my friends who work as copy editors have told me about the compulsion they feel to edit every piece of written material they see. A misspelled word in the newspaper will bring out the red pen, while awkward phrasing on a billboard results in a mental edit as they drive past. And if the email you send to your editor friend includes a comma splice—well, you know what happens next. It's like a switch they can't turn off.

Historians, I am obligated to report, have a similar affliction. We simply cannot resist the urge to correct factually imprecise statements about the past. Even when the facts themselves are correct—names, places, dates, etc.—an illogical or misinformed interpretation of historical events is simply too much to bear.

Governor Sean Parnell delivered his first "State of the State" address in January 2010, six sentences of which left me with an itch that just had to be scratched. The governor's words appear below in italics, interspersed with my historical analysis.

The United States' purchase of Alaska in 1867 began a relationship with the federal government, one that has at times been contentious. From the beginning, Alaska has been treated with skepticism from Outside. Every student knows the controversy inherent in the phrase "Seward's Folly."

But what every student might not know is that the "Seward's Folly" business is mostly bunk. Historian Richard Welch examined forty-eight of the country's largest newspapers of the time to ascertain their stance on the purchase of Alaska. He found that forty-four of them endorsed it, many with editorials that exhibited a more thorough understanding of the territory than one might expect. The U.S. Senate, for its part, approved the treaty by a procedural vote of 27 to 12, and a final vote of 37 to 2, margins that contradict the notion the purchase was unpopular. Those who argued against the purchase—and promulgated the "Seward's Folly" slander—did so largely for political reasons. William Seward had many enemies.

So why does the tale persist? Why has it become such an integral part of Alaska's accepted historical narrative? Historian Stephen Haycox: "It contributes to a standard interpretation...that Alaska has been through-out its history a victim. It has been misunderstood and mismanaged by a federal government [that] did not know Alaska conditions and yet presumed to act for it rather than letting Alaskans run their own affairs. The unpopularity tale suggests that the misunderstanding of Alaska goes back to the very beginning of the region's modern history."

Governor Sean Parnell delivers his State of the State Address to a joint session of the legislature in January 2010. OFFICE OF THE GOVERNOR, STATE OF ALASKA

In other words, the oft-repeated "Seward's Folly" story implies that no one but Alaskans really understand how the state should be managed. The feds? They don't have a clue. Never have.

Years later, Congress debated whether Alaska could support itself as a state.

Well, actually no. Congress debated whether Alaska should *be* a state. The distinction is important. Its ability to support itself economically was just one part of a very complex discussion. Alaska's strategic location at the height of the Cold War, for example, was but one issue that figured in the debate. Fish and game management was another. Corporate taxes and outside investment. Native land claims. A statehood land grant that would surely be larger than most states themselves, except Texas and maybe California. One of the more contentious issues was raised by Southern Democrats who feared Alaska's two new senators might support civil rights legislation. It was these types of arguments, some of which had nothing to do with Alaska itself and the people who lived there, that drove the debate.

So the governor's glib assertion that Congress cared only whether Alaska could "support itself" oversimplifies the issue. It suggests Alaskans were right and the skeptics have been proven wrong. (They doubted us, we drilled for oil, and now we're rich—statehood is vindicated!) The governor's revisionist phrasing supports the notion that because resource development is what secured our post-statehood destiny, *even more* resource development—managed of course by Alaskans who always know best—is the key to our future. I have no quarrel with this as a political position, but the governor's historical justification is incomplete.

With statehood, the strong assumption prevailed that, as a fledgling state, we would be allowed to develop our own resources without constant federal interference.

Parnell misunderstands that the statehood act is not the unbreakable compact he and so many others think it is. Statehood was not a free-for-all where Congress blithely handed over the keys to whomever happened to be living in Alaska at the time. The national interest was (and remains) in play. When the selection of state lands in the 1960s appeared to encroach on what Alaska Natives believed were their ancestral lands, for example, the Interior Department stepped in and halted the process until the Natives' claims could be resolved. By the same token, when the federal government determines that a national park or wildlife refuge is in the nation's interest it has the right to create it. When the U.S. Fish and Wildlife Service finds that a species of animal is threatened with extinction, it has the authority to take steps to prevent it. These actions might infuriate some Alaskans, especially those boosters who want unrestricted access to drill, mine, and harvest, and may also reinforce the long-standing feelings of victimization, but they do not constitute a betrayal of the statehood act.

We best realize statehood's promise and grow our economy when we determine our destiny—not Washington.

Governor Parnell's speech, or at least the select quotations offered here, taps into a mythology that goes back 150 years. It is the myth of

Alaskan exceptionalism. It is the story of self-reliant, hardscrabble pioneers who entered a wild frontier and, through hard work and force of will alone, built a new society better than those they left behind. According to the myth, they accomplished this feat in spite of the federal government, which alternately ignored them and provided no assistance, or micromanaged their newfound paradise with silly laws and ill-conceived regulations that constrained their right to live as they chose.

The myth is useful in politics—officials from James Wickersham to Ernest Gruening to Wally Hickel to Sean Parnell have used the theme of victimization to great electoral success—but it ignores the fact that Washington has supported Alaska in ways almost too numerous to list. But here are a few: subsidized mail delivery, weather forecasting, telecommunications, firefighting, U.S. Coast Guard, military spending, Homestead Act, Alaska Railroad, University of Alaska, the formation of judicial districts and a territorial legislature, health and education funding for Native tribes, road construction and maintenance, fisheries protection, unemployment insurance, Social Security, New Deal construction programs, Matanuska Colony, the 90/10 revenue split on federal lands, and finally, Uncle Ted money.

Professor Haycox writes of the myth's downside: "Its continuing legacy is a profound, disabling myopia which prevents present-day believers from seeing that they are victims only of a false egoism which once characterized American westward expansion." Alaskan exceptionalism teaches us that we are unique, that we are special, that conventional rules do not apply to us ("We don't give a damn how they do it Outside"). Yet a careful historical analysis shows that our political, economic, and social institutions are really no different from those that have developed in frontier areas throughout history, especially the American West in the late nineteenth century, again with inestimable assistance from the federal government.

Historical analysis can sometimes shatter myths. Facts have a way of interfering with our desired identities and beliefs. Although this sort of self-examination may be uncomfortable, it is really the only way to truly grasp our present situation in all its complexity. History is like a friend who is always honest, who tells you the good *and* the bad. The decision on whether or not to listen is up to you.

◆◆◆◆◆

I was in attendance at the 1998 public hearing in Fairbanks mentioned in this column where the National Park Service heard testimony on the proposed snowmachine ban in certain sections of Denali. A more surreal experience I'm not sure I've had. If you had just wandered in off the street and didn't know the topic of the hearing, you would've had a tough time figuring out just what was going on. There was lots of yelling and catcalls. One speaker might have mentioned air pollution, while the next claimed his civil rights were being violated. When the next three speakers referred to wildlife habitat for marmots, Congressional (mis)representation, and the noise difference between a 2- and 4-stroke engine, you likely would have found yourself thoroughly confused. That's the nature of land policy debates in Alaska. We're all arguing different facets of the often unknowable whole.

EVERY WINTER, USUALLY around November or December, the National Park Service opens certain sections of Denali National Park to snowmachines. The announcement comes when the snow cover in those areas reaches a level sufficiently robust to protect the tundra underneath. Some two million acres in the heart of the park, however, remain off limits on a permanent basis regardless of the amount of snow.

The NPS authority to alternately allow and restrict motorized access to different sections of Denali derives from the very 1917 legislation that created the park as well as subsequent rule-making processes that have evolved in concert with different user demands. The regulations may look simple on paper, but have never failed to stir passionate debate.

Indeed, a close examination of the Denali snowmachine controversy reveals it is about much, much more than Denali and snowmachines.

When Congress established Mount McKinley National Park in 1917, primarily as a wildlife refuge, it also authorized "recreation purposes" for the public. In winter this meant skiing and snowshoeing, with backcountry access largely limited to dogsled. For the first six decades of the park's existence the subject of snowmachines never came up. They were heavy, clunky, prone to frequent breakdowns, and simply unreliable as a means of backcountry transportation.

In 1980, the Alaska National Interest Lands Conservation Act (ANILCA) added four million acres to the park and renamed it Denali. The law, in its section on public recreation, authorized motorized access for the purpose of engaging in "traditional activities," such as fishing, trapping, and berry picking. The NPS still believed snowmachines would have minimal environmental impact as they required no permanent facilities and remained incapable of bringing large numbers of people into the park.

Over the next several years, of course, snowmachine technology advanced to the point where riders could go just about anywhere. Their primary function also began to shift from a purely utilitarian means of winter transportation to a recreational activity in and of itself. Citing the potential for adverse environmental impact, the NPS in 1998 proposed a ban on snowmachines in the two million-acre core that was once Mount McKinley Park.

The subsequent public process followed a predictable course in that wilderness advocates cheered while the snow-goers cried foul. What made the occasion unique was how the two sides appeared to be arguing dif-

Snowmachine of a bygone era. ROSS COEN

ferent issues altogether, a hallmark of land management debates through-out Alaska's history.

The Wilderness Society and other conservation groups supported the closure on the grounds it protected the solitude and natural quiet of the backcountry. The groups' only complaint was that the NPS hadn't gone far enough and should ban snowmachines from the entire park, at least until the true environmental impact could be ascertained. Environmental groups making environmental arguments—no surprise there.

The Alaska State Snowmobile Association (ASSA), however, largely sidestepped every environmental concern and framed the issue as an infringement on its members' rights. "This will become a national or even international issue," predicted a member of Fairbanks Snow Travelers, another interest group. "The bottom line is that it is a state's rights issue." In the eyes of the snowmachiners, theirs was a recreational activity like any other. The closure represented not an effort to protect a wondrous ecosystem but an attack on their lifestyle. The snowmachine groups began a statewide search for someone—anyone—who had ridden in the park prior to 1980. Establishing a legacy of personal use took primacy over (and might very well trump) any environmental arguments.

Snow-go enthusiasts stuck to this theme in a series of public hearings held around the state. "The conception that people don't use the area is just asinine," stated one rider at the Fairbanks hearing. What good is a wilderness area, went the argument, if people aren't allowed to enjoy it? Many who testified objected to the definition of "traditional activities," which did not include sightseeing or camping, the very pursuits of every snowmachiner who wanted to enter the park. The ASSA would later make these same arguments in a lawsuit alleging the Park Service violated ANILCA's motorized access provision and failed to consider alternatives that would protect recreational resources for all users. The environment figured into the ASSA platform only to the extent that no one, according to its lawsuit, could prove snowmachines had any negative impact.

The Denali snowmachine debate came to resemble so many others in the history of land use conflicts in Alaska, none more than the heated disputes over ANILCA itself in the late 1970s. President Jimmy Carter, to the delight of environmentalists everywhere, withdrew millions of acres of land for parks and refuges. Opponents called it a "lock-up" that betrayed the statehood act. Protesters in Fairbanks burned Carter in effigy. Much the way greenies and snow-goers would argue different sides of the Denali issue years later, Alaskans in the 1970s yelled past one another in a manner that suggested each group occupied the wrong public hearing room but didn't realize it. One side talked about wilderness and rivers and wolves; the other spoke of jobs and rights and personal freedoms.

Indeed, pick your lands controversy from Alaska's history—the Guggenheim coal interests, Rampart Dam, logging in the Tongass, Project

Chariot, Native land claims, Trans-Alaska Pipeline, Pebble Mine, and more—and chances are you'll find one group talking apples while the other refers only to oranges.

In the end, the old Mount McKinley Park remained closed to motorized vehicles, the four million-acre ANILCA additions stayed open, and park officials and snowmachiners agreed to good-faith negotiations on any future regulations. Everyone got something, and no one got everything—which is a pretty good summary of Alaska history in general.

a
DAY
for the
EARTH

♦♦♦♦♦

Historian Adam Rome has called the first Earth Day "the most famous little-known event in modern U.S. history." Far more people participated in Earth Day than in any civil rights march or antiwar demonstration of the time, Rome notes, yet the events of April 1970 are viewed today mostly as a footnote to the larger environmental movement. Rome suggests Earth Day was actually a catalyst for the movement itself. Dozens (perhaps hundreds) of environmental groups formed in 1970 remained active for years afterward, and many of the student activists at the first Earth Day are still working on environmental issues four decades later. The legacy of Earth Day is almost certainly larger than any of us realize.

GAYLORD NELSON, THE junior senator from Wisconsin, was on an airplane somewhere over California in January 1969, when a simple but brilliant idea popped into his head. Earlier that day he had visited the site of a major oil spill in Santa Barbara and was now reading a magazine article about "teach-ins," a new type of grassroots movement then happening on college campuses around the country designed to educate people about the war in Vietnam. What if students organized teach-ins on the environment, he wondered? What if they coordinated the events at dozens or even hundreds of communities on the exact same day?

"If we could tap into the environmental concerns of the general public and infuse the student anti-war energy into the environmental cause," Nelson later wrote, "we could generate a demonstration that would force the issue onto the national political agenda."

Earth Day was born.

On April 22, 1970, Americans from every walk of life and numbering in the millions (the exact total can only be guessed at) took action on behalf of the environment. They held festivals, workshops, and seminars. They took field trips and went on hikes. They picked up trash. And in the end, they accomplished just what Senator Nelson envisioned—they inserted environmental issues into the national discussion.

The Earth Day events that took place in Fairbanks resembled so many others across the country—film screenings at the university, lectures on ecology, and so on—but stood out on the national stage for the presence of the teach-in's keynote speaker who delivered an address on one of the most hot-button environmental issues of the day: Wally Hickel came to town to talk about the proposed trans-Alaska pipeline.

Hickel was then Secretary of the Interior under President Richard Nixon, a post he assumed after serving two years as Alaska's governor. A land developer and pro-development politician at heart, Hickel nonetheless professed an environmental sensibility and willingly engaged those who wanted to speak about ecology. After receiving dozens of invitations to Earth Day events around the country, Hickel agreed to appear at the University of Alaska where he would announce his decision on the oil companies' right-of-way application for the pipeline.

Although discussion of a resource development megaproject might have seemed out of place at an event focused on the environment, students on the local organizing committee welcomed the debate. They billed the teach-in as "an exploration of issues, not a protest; an awakening of concern, not a final prophecy of doom." The students' fair-minded approach won plaudits from many locals who appreciated the balanced program. Even the pro-development *Fairbanks Daily News-Miner* con-

Walter Hickel DAVID NORTON

Donald Aitken DAVID NORTON

gratulated the Earth Day committee for providing "a great opportunity to hear both sides of the issues so vital to us."

Joe Vogler was having none of it, however. In a scathing letter that appeared in the newspaper a few days before the teach-in, the miner and secessionist wrote, "To destroy the initiative which developed [the U.S.] they now scream ecology, environment, and are using our very constitutional safeguards to stop us dead in the water." Vogler equated environmentalists with snakes, enemies of the state, and of course Communists (he helpfully noted Earth Day was scheduled on the hundredth anniversary of Lenin's birth). "Come alive, America," he warned, "or you will be dead in the same living death you can see in the stagnation of people and progress in Russia, China, or Cuba."

Despite Vogler's warning, or perhaps because of it, some seven hundred people packed the university gymnasium for a program that featured Hickel and Donald Aitken, a professor of physics at Stanford University. Aitken opened the program with an address that cautioned against a mad rush toward economic development. The oil industry's plans for the pipeline, he claimed, were moving faster than its knowledge of how to build it safely or anyone's ability to grasp the true environmental impact. Stated Aitken: "The scientific data are only now becoming available [and] since we really don't know we make wild guesses and plunge blindly ahead." He issued a harsh rebuke to state officials, especially Governor Keith Miller, for their haste in trying to get the pipeline built.

Wally Hickel then took the podium and made the long-awaited declaration everyone expected: "I am announcing tonight that I will issue the permit for the pipeline right-of-way." He stated his determination to make the project a "showcase" that would prove how enlightened development and environmental practices could go hand-in-hand. Construction of the 800-mile pipeline would not actually begin for another four years until Native land claims and environmental litigation had been resolved, but as far as the Interior Department was concerned the pipeline proposal was on track to satisfy all technical requirements.

"I can guarantee that we will not approve any design based on the faulty concept of 'build now, repair later.'" It was a favorite phrase of Hickel's, one that he repeated many times in print and speeches about the pipeline. It also represented a general operating principle he brought to all resource development debates. Whether permafrost or wildlife habitat or any of a thousand other issues, Hickel emphasized the question was never *if* development should proceed, but rather *how*. The sentiment displeased many teach-in attendees who believed the option of not building the pipeline at all should be considered. One reporter covering the event noted that not everyone clapped at the conclusion of Hickel's speech and only a few stood up.

If the overall intent of Earth Day was to bring nationwide attention to environmental concerns, Alaska showed itself already ahead of the game. Hickel's speech was national news and the tug-of-war between developers and conservationists, between oil drilling and the wilderness, would dominate national discussion for years. The pipeline would be the subject of the first Environmental Impact Statement prepared as a result

Interior Secretary Walter Hickel (second from left) tours a polluted section of the Chena River on Earth Day. Joining Hickel are (left to right) David Norton, Ron Gordon, and Harold Dinkins. JOHN METZGER, POLAR STAR / SUN STAR

of the National Environmental Policy Act passed by Congress that year. Alaska was then and remains today the backdrop for all manner of environmental debates. The characters in this melodrama change over time, but history has shown that no matter the environmental issue there will always be a letter in the newspaper like that written by Mr. Vogler, there will always be a skeptic like Dr. Aitken, there will always be a booster like Secretary Hickel, and there will always an audience of Alaskans, some of whom clap and some of whom don't.

COUNTING
ALASKA

◆◆◆◆◆

The 2010 Census officially began on January 25 in the community of Noorvik, Alaska, where census director Robert Groves traveled by dogsled and conducted the very first enumeration in the country. "Today we begin the largest domestic undertaking in our nation's history," he stated. "Getting an accurate count here will set the standard for the rest of the country." The visit to the northwest Alaska community of 650 people was largely a publicity stunt to generate interest nationwide. The Census Bureau did note, however, that counting in rural Alaska always starts early in order to catch residents at home before they leave for spring hunting or warm-weather jobs. This column, which ran in May 2010, describes the challenges faced by Mr. Groves's predecessors a century before.

IT'S THAT TIME of the decade again.

Enumerators from the U.S. Census Bureau are canvassing neighborhoods across the country in an effort to count every single one of us (or at least those who didn't count themselves with the mail-in form). Nowadays the challenges the census agents are most likely to encounter include unfriendly dogs and even more unfriendly people who, for whatever reason, wish to remain uncounted and see the federal employee with the clipboard vacate their property forthwith. (It probably goes without saying Alaska has an abundance of both species of creature.)

A century ago, however, employees of the Census Bureau in Alaska faced hardships orders of magnitude greater in number and severity. That the official report on the 1910 census made special note of the fact no enumerators *died* in the discharge of their duty suggests it was a rough go indeed.

"I left Valdez on March 12, 1910," wrote an enumerator for the Third Census District (everything south of the Alaska Range and north of the panhandle), "and proceeded by dog teams with about 1,000 pounds of provisions over Thompson Pass." In order to count the many men then building the Copper River railroad, the enumerator had to negotiate the river's deep, swift channels and scale what he called "precipitous cliffs from 100 to 200 feet high." His travels also took him through the deep snow of the mountains where laborers were cutting ties and timber for the railroad. The agent returned to Valdez after two months on the trail and, incredibly, closed his report by noting, "There were no special difficulties encountered in this work."

The agent in charge of the Nome office reported a particularly harsh winter on the Seward Peninsula: "Besides the unusually low temperature the winter was an endless series of severe blizzards." Several area residents froze to death, he noted. The Fairbanks district likewise experienced brutal winter conditions, as evidenced by the travails of an enumerator in Chandalar. "At no time after he left Fairbanks did the thermometer rise above 30 degrees below zero. Two of his dogs froze to death, and he himself froze portions of his face several times, and at one time dropped into six feet of open water, nearly losing his life."

One census worker came upon a remote cabin and found its occupant with a severe case of frostbite. The man "had frozen his fingers, and had himself cut off one gangrenous member with his knife." In transporting the man to the nearest village, one member of the party stepped into water and soaked his foot. The appendage froze and turned black, but

Census enumerator Agnes Farnsworth (right) with the John family in Barrow (c. 1950). WARD WELLS, WIEN COLLECTION, ANCHORAGE MUSEUM, B85.27.970

the man recovered. (I suspect census officials in Washington, D.C. found the Alaska reports exponentially more fascinating than those from, say, Delaware.)

The Census Bureau had decided to conduct its Alaska operation in wintertime for several reasons.

First, the thick forests and marshy tundra made travel across the roadless territory virtually impossible in the summer months. Not only would any residents away from the navigable waterways likely remain uncounted, but attempting to reach them would require many more enumerators and break the budget of the operation. The Bureau further noted that nearly every able-bodied man and woman in the country spent the summers mining for gold or building cabins or laboring at some other project. Securing a workforce for the census at that time would be difficult and could only be accomplished by offering wages two or three times what men would settle for in the winter. Finally, it was believed that the many thousands of people who flocked to Alaska every summer did not count as "bona fide" residents. Few had any intention of making Alaska their home, but instead headed back south with the first hard freeze every autumn. They would be counted there.

Enumerators in 1910 found the Tanana Valley a very different place from ten years before when a relatively sparse population in well-defined camps proved easy to count. The 1900 record lists barely 2,000 souls and only nine villages that qualified as population units. Ten years later they found eight times as many people distributed up and down every creek in the region. They also identified forty-eight distinct towns, villages, and settlements. The population of Alaska as a whole, however, remained virtually unchanged from the previous census, rising just 1.2 percent to 64,356 residents.

The 1910 census was the first in Alaska to go beyond a simple count (enumerators in 1900, for example, were known to look at ship manifests and simply guess). This time they recorded comprehensive demographic data in a range of categories including race, ethnicity, parentage, place of birth, country of origin, school attendance and literacy, and numbers of families and dwellings in different regions. The diligence shown by the Census Bureau corresponded to a general upsurge in attention by the federal government. The formation of judicial districts that decade led to formal legal authority where none previously existed, while imminent acts of Congress would soon grant territorial status and establish an elected legislature—all of which required an accurate count of Alaska residents. Federal appropriations also depended on the number of people in the territory, which, then as now, probably remained the most convincing argument to allow oneself to be counted.

SEVERE DAYS
on the
COPPER
and the
TANANA

•••••

Henry Tureman Allen, an ambitious young army officer in 1885, seemed an unlikely candidate to lead one of the most accomplished explorations of Alaska, as historian Morgan Sherwood pointed out: "He was neither blunt nor sharp-tongued, and the seeming lack of stern qualities made other officers doubt that he possessed command ability. Moreover, he was tall, direct, handsome, and meticulous in his dress, with a pleasant manner and distinguished military bearing that made him a favorite with the ladies." Nevertheless, Allen actively sought the Alaska assignment and proved himself an unparalleled leader and explorer.

"BY AUTHORITY OF the Lieutenant General of the Army…Second Lieutenant Henry T. Allen, Second Cavalry, acting aide-de-camp, is authorized to make a reconnaissance in Alaska, proceeding up the Copper River and down the Tanana River Valley."

This simple order, conveyed by the U.S. Army's Department of the Columbia on January 27, 1885, marked the beginning of one of the most amazing feats of exploration ever to occur in Alaska. A three-man team led by Lieutenant Allen completed a 1,500-mile traverse that took them along the two aforementioned rivers as well as the Yukon. Along the way they mapped territory no western explorer had ever seen.

If the expedition looked on paper to be a simple matter of floating down a few rivers, the reality in 1885 was that every previous effort to penetrate the Copper River region had ended in failure, if not utter disaster. The Russians had tried several times going as far back as the late 1700s (their last attempt ended with the deaths of twelve men at the hands of hostile natives). Two American expeditions launched following the 1867 purchase of Alaska also failed to explore the region.

The Tanana, for its part, was the Copper's equal in terms of mystery. William Healey Dall, at the time the acknowledged expert on Alaskan exploration, once floated the Yukon past its confluence with the Tanana and, gazing up the murky river, noted that "no white man has dipped his paddle" into its waters. So little was known of the deep Interior that the very source of the Tanana's waters could only be guessed at.

Lt. Allen arrived in Nuchek, an outpost on Hinchinbrook Island opposite the Copper River Delta, on March 19, 1885, aboard a small U.S. Navy man-of-war called the *Pinta*. In preparing for the expedition, the young officer had read every published account of previous Alaskan explorations. The last attempt on the Copper River—that of William Abercrombie just the year before—had failed in part due to an oversized expeditionary force that was burdened with several tons of supplies. Accordingly, Allen insisted on a small team that could nimbly adapt to whatever conditions lay ahead. His official orders set the expedition's size at just three men, with additional laborers (white and native) to be hired along the way if necessary.

"We left Nuchek for the mouth of the Copper River," reads the first line of Allen's narrative, "in the two boats obtained from the natives, with crews consisting of four white men and three natives." The team proceeded up the Copper, though rough water and floating ice required them to haul out frequently and portage on land. Sleds loaded with hundreds of pounds of gear now punched through the soft snow, so the men ditched nearly everything but what they could carry on their backs.

Lieutenant Henry T. Allen (center) in St. Michael, Alaska, at the conclusion of the Copper and Tanana Rivers Expedition, August 1885. Allen is flanked by Private Fred Fickett (left) and Sergeant Cady Robertson (right, misidentified as "Robinson" in the original caption). FRED WILSON FICKETT PAPERS, UAA-HMC-0108-SERIES8B-1, ARCHIVES AND SPECIAL COLLECTIONS, CONSORTIUM LIBRARY, UNIVERSITY OF ALASKA ANCHORAGE

For the next few weeks the men trudged through rain and snow, their clothing perpetually soaked, their food stores running low. On one cold evening no member of the team could successfully light a match. "These days were severe ones," wrote Allen, "but an excellent discipline for the even more trying work that was soon to follow."

Finding it difficult to make forward progress and hunt game at the same time, Allen encouraged his men to make economic use of every animal they took. "At this time we made the first attempt at eating the entrails of an animal—a porcupine," he wrote on April 7. "They were not relished," he dryly noted. Before long the men were also consuming maggot-infested moose meat. Their first contact with natives a week later resulted in a celebration with enough food that the men were able to satisfy their hunger for the first time since the start of the voyage.

Seven weeks later, after receiving inestimable assistance from the region's indigenous peoples and literally pulling their boats with ropes up the length of the Copper, Allen and his men arrived at a pass in the Alaska Range he named for General Nelson Miles (today known as Suslota Pass). In the early morning hours of June 9 he scaled a snow-capped ridge and, under the light of the midnight sun, saw before him a remarkable vista:

> *The views in advance and in rear were both grand; the former showing the extensive Tanana Valley with numerous lakes and the low unbroken range of mountains between the Tanana and Yukon Rivers. On this pass, with both white and yellow buttercups around me and snow within a few feet, I sat proud of the grand sight which no visitor save an Atnatana or Tananatana had ever seen.*

Any precipitation that fell upon that ridge, Allen knew, would by chance enter the Copper watershed to the south and eventually flow into Prince William Sound, or run to the north into the Tanana, then the Yukon, and finally to the Bering Sea. The first phase of his mission was complete. He was leaving the Copper and entering the Tanana—the first white man, as he noted, ever to do so.

Allen first contemplated a raft for the Tanana, but was dissuaded by natives at Tetlin who told him such a craft would be inappropriate for the rapids and logjams to come. The team instead built a caribou-skin boat and made a dash for the Yukon. Covering as many as fifty river miles a day, they traversed the Tanana in just two weeks. (On June 20, while floating the section of river closest to where Fairbanks would be founded seventeen years later, Allen wrote only that "large masses of driftwood and sunken soil, with its vegetation partly submerged, were passed.") After hasty excursions up the Kanuti and Koyukuk rivers, Allen closed the season by following the Yukon to Nulato and portaging to St. Michael where passage back to the south was arranged.

It's no exaggeration to say that when Lieutenant Allen set off from the mouth of the Copper that spring the Alaskan Interior represented one of the last great blank spots on the map of North America. Not only did he fill that gap with maps that proved remarkably accurate, especially considering the pace with which he moved through the territory, but he also laid the foundation for the many scientific and commercial expeditions that followed. That few Alaskans today know the name Henry T. Allen is a shame. On the list of the most incredible wilderness expeditions ever to take place in Alaska, his certainly stands near the top.

THE GOVERNOR, HIS DEPUTY,
and a
SWEETHEART DEAL GONE SOUR

·····

Bill Sheffield seemed to be in hot water from the moment he was elected governor in 1982. His first scandal involved a string of campaign fundraisers hosted by oil executives— conspicuously held immediately after the governor announced an oil lease sale in Norton Sound. He also accepted a $100,000 loan from an Anchorage businessman, then wrote a $100,000 personal check to his campaign fund the very next day. More controversy followed when it was revealed that every hotel and catering contract from the governor's office—some $27,500 in food, liquor, and entertainment—went to businesses owned or operated by Sheffield. In retrospect, these relatively minor scandals were just the warm-up for the big-time blunder that nearly brought down Sheffield's administration.

"THE GRAND JURY believes, based on the evidence presented during this investigation, that the [William] Sheffield Administration has not best served the interests of the public and is unfit to fulfill the inherent duties of public office."

So wrote ten women and five men serving on a grand jury in Juneau on July 2, 1985. The panel's 69-page report then launched an event unprecedented in the state's history—gubernatorial impeachment hearings against Governor Bill Sheffield.

Governor Bill Sheffield (second from right) with his attorneys following the decision by the Alaska State Senate not to pursue impeachment, August 5, 1985. ANCHORAGE DAILY NEWS/MCT/LANDOV

The sequence of events that led to the showdown started, as scandals often do, with a campaign contributor visiting the State Capitol.

In October 1984, Lenny Arsenault, a labor leader who had raised $92,000 in campaign funds for Sheffield, met with the governor and his chief of staff, John Shively. The state was about to issue a request for competitive bids on new office space in Fairbanks. Arsenault, who had obtained a draft copy of the bid documents from Sheffield, asked the governor to revise the specifications in such a way that only one building—Arsenault's—would qualify for the $9 million contract. The request for bids was scrapped shortly thereafter and the state signed a sole-source contract with Arsenault's company.

But as with so many other political scandals, it wasn't so much the deed itself that caused trouble but the cover-up that followed. Acting on a tip, a reporter called Shively and starting asking questions about the contract. Shively stonewalled the reporter. He then took the file from his drawer and dumped it in the trash.

The whole story came out later, but only after Shively first lied to investigators (he claimed to have no idea what happened to the file or how Arsenault got a copy of the bid specifications). He escaped charges of perjury only because he wasn't under oath at the time. When Gov. Sheffield testified before the grand jury he claimed to not even remember meeting with Arsenault. At times the whole affair resembled a bad spy movie: Shively enlisted an aide to call Arsenault and warn him of the pending investigation, but ordered her to leave the Capitol and make the call from a pay phone down the street.

After calling forty-four witnesses and examining thousands of pages of records, jurors concluded no criminal indictments against Sheffield and Shively were warranted, but that their conduct proved them unfit to hold office. The panel made particular note of Sheffield's "lack of candor" in answering its questions. The ball then shifted to the State Senate's court where legislators took up the question of impeachment.

"The whole thing is unbelievable to me," said a defiant Sheffield. Shively, who acknowledged his wrongdoing and would eventually resign, also expressed bewilderment at the process: "It's sort of hard for me to believe they went through nine or ten weeks of investigation, found no criminal activity, and then recommended impeachment."

In testifying before the Senate Rules Committee, Sheffield reiterated that he simply did not recall discussing the office lease with Arsenault. The governor is a busy executive, his lawyer told legislators, and he cannot be expected to remember every single meeting. The argument held little sway with the Rules Committee, which noted Sheffield "exhibited almost verbatim recall of conversations and events that were favorable to him and a substantial lack of recall of events that might reflect upon him unfavorably."

Despite its skepticism, the Senate voted against impeachment. While most everyone agreed the actions of the governor did not meet appropriate standards of integrity, his removal from office was deemed too harsh a penalty. The unwritten code of politics also came into play: don't vote against a colleague for something you yourself—helping a campaign contributor—have also done.

Today, a quarter century later, the truly remarkable thing about the scandal is just what little effect it had on the careers of Sheffield and Shively. The former improperly granted a juicy contract to a political contributor and then dissembled about his role in the affair, while the latter lied to a grand jury and destroyed evidence in an attempt to cover it up. The modern political landscape is littered with ruined reputations of public officials who did a lot less—yet both Sheffield and Shively walked away from the scandal and went on to prestigious public careers.

After leaving office in 1986, Bill Sheffield headed the Alaska Railroad for many years and today is director of the Port of Anchorage. He has attained the status of revered elder statesman whose counsel is sought on a range of policy issues. The embarrassing impeachment business is almost never mentioned.

John Shively, for his part, reentered state government in 1995 as Commissioner of Natural Resources in the Tony Knowles administration and today chairs the Pebble Partnership, a high-profile resource development consortium. In 2009, the Alaska Chamber of Commerce presented Shively with its "Outstanding Alaskan of the Year" award.

It's often said that Alaska is a place where you can leave your past behind. Reinvent yourself even. One need only look at the two men at the center of the state's only gubernatorial impeachment hearing to know that's true.

ONE PERSON, ONE VOTE

38

❖❖❖❖

*This column appeared in September 2010, just before the
election at which voters overwhelmingly rejected the proposed
increase to the size of the Alaska legislature. Identifying
reasons for the measure's defeat is problematic—there was no
organized campaign against it, and it received so little media
attention both before and after the election that political
watchers can only speculate on the electorate's motives. It
seems reasonable to argue, however, that the prospects for
Ballot Measure #1 were doomed for two reasons. First, in a
fundamentally conservative state like Alaska, the "no" vote
almost always has a built-in advantage no matter the issue
in question. Second, the addition of six new members to the
legislature carried a price tag in the millions. This was the
wrong year to ask Alaskans to cough up some dough to expand
the size of government.*

RURAL ALASKA IS almost sure to lose legislative representation in 2012
when district lines are redrawn following this year's census. While population has increased in certain urban areas (the Mat-Su, for one) rural
districts have lost residents in the last ten years. With the number of
legislators constitutionally set at 40 in the House and 20 in the Senate, at
least one seat and possibly more currently based in rural Alaska will shift

to urban centers. Those remaining rural districts will then have to grow even larger in size to garner the requisite number of constituents.

Unless voters approve Ballot Measure #1, that is.

Officially named "An Act to Increase Number of Legislators and Districts," the measure would expand the Senate from 20 to 22 members and the House from 40 to 44 members, and would create six new legislative districts. The expansion of both chambers would preserve the number of rural legislators.

Tinkering with the very structure of government may seem bold and unprecedented, yet it has happened in Alaska more often than you might think. On several previous occasions Alaskans have altered the form and function of the legislative branch, often in response to changing political circumstances.

An overview of those occasions might help to place the current debate in context.

Congress established the territorial legislature with the Second Organic Act of 1912. Although its authority was purposefully limited by a federal government reluctant to cede any real power, Alaskans embraced this new form of home rule. The House had sixteen members, while the Senate contained eight. But because apportionment was based on the territory's four judicial districts and not on population, a handful of legislators representing just a fraction of Alaska residents could stymie all legislative efforts. The system worked well for the salmon packers and other Outside companies who needed only a few key members in their pocket in order to run the show in Juneau—or bring the show to a complete standstill, as was often the case.

When Ernest Gruening arrived in Alaska in 1939 as the new territorial governor he recognized the disadvantage of a small legislature. His plans to revise the tax code would certainly not pass until the size and method of apportionment were changed. Steady population growth in Southcentral and the Interior required a system of proportional representation, Gruening believed, with district boundaries that could be redrawn periodically to reflect changes in population.

John Hellenthal, delegate to the Alaska Constitutional Convention, who chaired the committee that set rules for apportionment and legislative representation. CONSTITUTIONAL CONVENTION DELEGATE PHOTOGRAPHS, UAF-1983-185-28, ALASKA AND POLAR REGIONS, RASMUSON LIBRARY, UNIVERSITY OF ALASKA FAIRBANKS

Alaska's congressional delegate Anthony Dimond agreed, and in late 1942 he engineered an amendment to the Organic Act that doubled the size of the senate to 16 members, increased the number of representatives to 24, and established a revisable system of apportionment more closely tied to population. This change, which took effect in 1945, allowed Gruening to break the lobbyists' stranglehold and advance his legislative agenda.

A decade later delegates to the Alaska Constitutional Convention met in Fairbanks and set about writing a founding document for the future state. On the question of legislative representation, a few favored keeping things as they were in the territorial body—16 in the Senate, 24 in the House—while others again recognized that the relatively small chambers would always be susceptible to the whims of a few obstructionists. They recommended expanding the membership.

John Hellenthal, chair of the convention's apportionment committee, introduced his report on January 11, 1956, with a knowing comment on the controversy sure to follow: "I don't think if you were given the problem of apportioning the heavens that you could please all of the occupants, but you just have to try."

The committee's proposal called for 40 members in the House, one each from 24 districts with the balance allocated from those areas with more residents. With Alaska's population then numbering 203,000, each member would represent about 5,000 people. Hellenthal noted the committee had studied other state legislatures, especially those in large western states that similarly featured a low population scattered over a wide geographical area, and determined 40 members would ensure adequate and equitable representation. He called it a "wieldy" number.

Membership in the Senate, on the other hand, was to be half that of the House and would be based on geographic area. Much like in the U.S. Senate, the system would favor the districts with the lowest number of people (i.e., rural areas) at the expense of more densely populated cities. One senator from the bush might represent just 10,000 people, for example, while his colleague from Anchorage might have four times as many constituents. The proposal purposefully overrepresented rural districts in recognition that as Alaska's population grew—which it was certain to do in the decades following statehood—nearly all growth would occur in urban areas.

The U.S. Supreme Court struck down this system of weighted representation in two landmark rulings in the 1960s. Membership in state legislatures was now to be based on the principle of "one person, one vote." It was a perfectly equitable measure on paper but one that is impossible to achieve in Alaska without creating huge rural districts of the type we presently have. Such districts, however fairly apportioned, violate what the authors of our constitution called "the principle of compactness," where districts would be as compact and contiguous as possible, and should not contain communities with competing socioeconomic interests.

Although the number, shape, and means for reapportioning legislative districts have all changed since the beginning of statehood, the number of legislators has not. If convention delegates saw 5,000 constituents per legislator as "wieldy" in 1956, the current system where each member of the House represents some 17,000 Alaskans certainly merits a reexamination.

Alaskans have been willing to modify the structure of state government from time to time. Whether additional seats should now be added to the legislature is a decision Alaskans must consider with great care. History shows, however, that such a move would not be unprecedented.

from
the
DESK
of
JOE
VOGLER

✦✦✦✦✦

This two-part column appeared in October and November 2010, precisely when Tea Party candidates around the country rode a wave of populist rage to (some) electoral success. In Alaska, Tea Party poster boy Joe Miller shocked nearly everyone by outpolling Lisa Murkowski in the Senate primary. He did so largely by playing to voters' fears. An out-of-control federal government, Miller claimed, was ignoring the Constitution and threatening to bankrupt the country. Paranoia is a powerful force in politics. Miller was certainly not the first to use it in Alaska.

THE VERY FIRST issue of *The Ester Republic* hit newsstands in January 1999. I consider the timing unfortunate for no other reason than it means the late Joe Vogler, who died in 1993, never got to write a letter to the editor.

If given the chance, he would have had some choice words for the posy-sniffers in Ester, I assure you.

Joe Vogler arrived in Alaska in 1942, a time when individuals could homestead or otherwise acquire large plots of land and pretty much do as they pleased on it. He often said he left the Lower 48 because there were too many rules, too many people, and not enough opportunities for a man to be free. Once in Fairbanks, he became a miner and land developer who believed no one had any right to tell him what he could and couldn't do on his own property. He also started writing letters to the editor.

In the five decades Vogler lived in the Interior, he penned dozens of white-hot missives in the *Fairbanks Daily News-Miner*, in most cases proving unable to respect the 300-word limit imposed by the paper's editor. He is certainly not the most prolific letter writer in newspaper history. He usually sent in just one letter a year, maybe two. But his hyperbolic rhetoric and absolute certainty that he was right about everything made his postings memorable. They often generated half a dozen letters in response. You could always count on Joe to liven up page 4.

"Our leaders are political cowards," he wrote in a rambling tirade about gun control on July 10, 1968, "and they tremble before the vociferous and militant minorities of certain groups." Vogler went on to state his belief that those who favored gun control "do so because they foresee the day approaching when the people will rise up in righteous wrath and reestablish a government which will abide by the Constitution."

Writing in December 1963 in opposition to the formation of the Fairbanks borough, Vogler noted, "If just one voter allows his right to vote to be influenced by the by the dictatorial flavor of this election, our way of life has been damaged and threatened."

He saw despots and dictators everywhere he looked. "Freedom from tyranny is much more difficult to keep than it is to win in the hot fires of revolution," he wrote in February 1964. "Men too long abused and oppressed will always rise and throw off the shackles upon their rights."

A few common themes begin to emerge.

First, Vogler's rhetoric is steeped in revolution and the struggle against creeping despotism, but what he called tyranny was usually just someone with different political views. For Vogler, anyone who disagreed with him wasn't just wrong—they were dishonorable scoundrels who hated the Constitution and threatened the very survival of America. When the state legislature set out legal procedures for the formation of boroughs,

Joe Vogler CHARLES MASON

for example, he believed "the thinking behind this law was closely akin to that of Hitler and Mussolini." When Governor Bill Egan suggested in 1972 the state take an ownership share in the Trans-Alaska Pipeline, Vogler offered the idea must have come from his masters in the USSR.

Second, Vogler was a classic misanthrope in that he continually referred to an idealized past, to a time thirty (or three hundred) years ago when men were free and government hadn't yet figured out how to destroy the individual. It was not *he* who changed, nor was *he* the radical among us, but rather the rest of society had somehow lost its way. To say he distrusted humanity is an understatement.

Finally, and most obviously, Joe Vogler was a very angry man.

In December 1957, a "vandal and fence-busting swine" in search of a Christmas tree traipsed onto Vogler's property and cut one down. "Whoever butchered that nice spruce last Sunday had best keep clear of me or I might wreck his Merry Christmas under my heel in about the same fashion he clobbered my tree." To emphasize the point he noted, "I do not forgive and I do not forget."

Vogler reserved a special type of scorn for environmentalists, whom he usually referred to in the most pejorative terms. Writing in January 1966 in support of Rampart Dam, a proposed hydro mega-project on the Yukon River that would have flooded millions of acres, Vogler ridiculed the dam's opponents as "duck-loving posy-sniffers." In another letter he blasted federal land holdings, which he referred to as "just a big frozen park wherein only posy-sniffing, bug-hunting, bird-watching swine are now grunting." (The following week, a clever environmentalist pointed out the word "vogler" means "bird catcher" in German.)

Vogler is best remembered today as the founder of the Alaskan Independence Party, a secessionist group he launched in 1973 largely out of frustration with what he saw as the spinelessness of every public official in the state. Because Vogler put his political views so clearly on display in dozens of letters to the editor over the years, a review of those letters reveals a natural progression in his thinking that led him to establish the new party.

Let's take a look at that political evolution.

Following the Alaska Constitutional Convention of 1955-56, where delegates from around the territory authored the founding document of the future state, Vogler wrote in support of the general principle but in opposition to the article dealing with mining leases. "I have wished for statehood many times," he noted, "but I refuse to trade my right to prospect for a constitution which differs in this respect from…every other American state." Vogler was referring to the provision that required miners to obtain permits for the exclusive right of exploration on mineral lands. "Not one of the men who pioneered Alaska needed an exclusive prospecting lease," he claimed. "I believe that Felix Pedro and the thousands of other pioneers…will roll in their graves in disgust at this provision."

By proclaiming himself in support of statehood—but opposed to *this particular form* of statehood—Vogler was beginning to cast himself as a victimized minority whose only recourse, it would turn out, was to become a secessionist.

When the state legislature passed the Mandatory Borough Law in 1963, Vogler was incensed. "Let him [the bill's sponsor] explain how he or any other group know what is best for the residents of this area. Let him explain where and from whom he secured his mandate to dictate our form of government." He filed a lawsuit attempting to have the law declared unconstitutional. He lost in Superior Court and went right back to writing angry letters in which he railed against the tyranny of the majority.

The betrayals only continued.

In October 1970, Vogler blasted the *News-Miner* and the League of Women Voters for opposing the call to convene another constitutional convention: "Our constitution leaves much to be desired and to postpone its correction for another ten years is to compound its faults."

A recommendation by the Bureau of Land Management to prohibit homesteading on 19 million acres of reclassified land inspired Vogler to write, "Who do they think they are? Are they placing themselves upon the throne of judgment to rule that agriculture has no role in the future of Interior Alaska?" If Vogler didn't already hate the federal government by this point, he was well on his way.

The first sign of a new political party on the horizon came in a March 1972 letter from Vogler to Governor Bill Egan (reprinted in the newspaper) in which he blasted the idea of a property tax. "I suggest that Wally Hickel did a fine job of burying the Republican Party. Are you now ready to bury the Democratic Party with your medieval property tax? This could provide the spark of life…for the birth of a new third party in Alaska."

The following year Vogler began circulating a petition in order to test the independence waters: "We the undersigned residents of Alaska do hereby respectfully and without malice or rancor petition the President and the Congress…to grant us our land, free and independent sovereignty, under the auspices of the Nations, from this day forth." He ultimately claimed to have gathered 25,000 signatures (almost certainly an exaggeration).

Looking back, the campaign was surprising in many ways. For a man defined by his righteous anger, Vogler struck a modest tone. He disavowed the term "secession" for its rebellious connotations, instead calling for a peaceful separation by mutual agreement of both parties. He called it a "bumper sticker" campaign and claimed to have no great quarrel with the federal government. "I appreciate what the government has done for us," he explained. "I can't help but think we can do better ourselves."

If Vogler is remembered today as a fire-breathing radical who worked the extreme fringe of Alaska politics, it is worth noting the platform of the party he founded was not that dissimilar from mainstream political movements throughout Alaska's history. His was not the first campaign (nor the last) to use the specter of a federal power grab as a rallying call. Historian Terrence Cole has noted how Vogler's arguments for self-determination grew from the same tradition that inspired the Alaska statehood campaign two decades earlier. The two movements even used the same rhetoric.

In January 1974, in a move that underscores Vogler's mainstream approach, he wrote to Ernest Gruening, the former governor, senator, and most revered Alaska statesman at the time, to offer him the AIP chairmanship. "If I did not feel that it would be a gross imposition upon your energies," he wrote, "I would ask you to seriously consider stepping up to lead our Independence Movement." Referring to the statehood movement of the 1950s in which Gruening played a prominent role, Vogler wrote, "We are seeking the same thing that you were—the right to determine our own destiny." The 87-year old Gruening replied that he wasn't prepared to join Vogler's party yet, but that "total secession" remained an option as long as the federal government continued its abuse of Alaska.

Over the next two decades, of course, Vogler grew even more strident in his antipathy toward Washington. "The fires of hell are frozen glaciers compared to my hatred of the federal government," he famously barked. So great was his fury that following his death in 1993, and in accordance with his wishes, he was buried in Dawson City, Yukon. He refused to spend eternity resting under the American flag.

RENAMING
ALASKA

One of my favorite books is The Dictionary of Alaska Place Names *by Donald Orth. Find it at your local library, get comfortable on the sofa, crack it open—and watch four hours slip right by as you are unable to put it down.*

A PERSONAL STORY, if you'll indulge me.

My first brush with cynicism came as a fourth grader at Jefferson Elementary in Valley City, North Dakota. Our class took a field trip to the Barnes County History Museum, which was exciting at the time but now appears in my memory as really nothing more than a cramped, poorly ventilated room in the courthouse basement filled mostly with rusty farm tools that qualified as historical largely because they were old.

Our good teacher pointed out one artifact after another, then proudly held up an old, yellowed map of the county. She asked if anything looked amiss. I don't recall who noticed it first—I'd like to think it was me—but it was pointed out that Valley City, our hometown and the county seat, was labeled Worthington. That was the original name of the town, the curator explained, but it had to be changed when the post office figured out that another burg in the territory had claimed the name some months before.

211

I was crushed. This was my hometown, a place that at the worldly age of ten I believed was the center of the universe, and now it turned out that its very name was a second choice. Mine was a town with a built-in inferiority complex! Even worse, the name they chose—Valley City—wasn't even a proper name, but just a descriptor of its location at the bottom of a wide basin. Was creativity in that short supply in southeastern North Dakota in 1883?

Names clearly mean a lot. Our cultural identities are often tied up in names. Just ask a Russian how it feels to live in Leningrad as opposed to Saint Petersburg. The names Rhodesia and Zimbabwe refer to the same country in Africa, but hold vastly different connotations for the (white and black) people who live there. The body of water between Japan and Korea is called either—you guessed it—the Sea of Japan or the Korean (East) Sea depending on whom you ask.

Closer to home, the names Denali and Mount McKinley conjure different emotions even though both refer to the exact same place. Indeed, here in Alaska we have our share of name-induced identity crises.

The town of Harrisburg sprang up in Southeast Alaska when gold was discovered there in 1880. Named for Richard Harris, one of the two prospectors who made the strike, the town attracted thousands and quickly became the largest in the territory. But at a miner's meeting the following year, Harris's partner called for a name change and allegedly bribed enough residents to vote for his proposal. His name? Joe Juneau.

The transient nature of gold rush towns often led to confusion regarding their names. When miners looking for an overland route to the Klondike established Copper City in 1898, they overlooked the fact that Spanish explorer Don Salvador Fidalgo had been there a century before and named the port for Antonio Valdes y Basan. The local postmaster deferred to the Spaniards and changed the name back to Valdez.

In 1905, again following a gold strike, surveys began for a town on the Tanana River a hundred river miles upstream from Fairbanks. The news thrilled James Wickersham who recommended the town be named

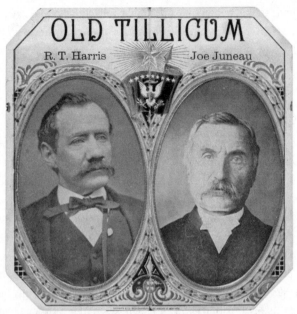

Cigar box label (c. 1900) featuring portraits of Richard Harris and Joe Juneau. Alaska's capital city might have been named for Harris were it not for the aggressive lobbying by his partner. RICHARD TIGHE HARRIS FAMILY PAPERS, UAA-HMC-0131-SERIES5B-59-2, ARCHIVES AND SPECIAL COLLECTIONS, CONSORTIUM LIBRARY, UNIVERSITY OF ALASKA ANCHORAGE

for his good friend, the recently departed Louis Sloss, who contributed to the opening of the frontier as first president of the Alaska Commercial Company. The locals ignored Wickersham, however, and named the town for Wilds P. Richardson, head of the Alaska Road Commission. The move no doubt pained the judge as he detested the man. The town is long since abandoned, but Richardson's name still graces the road he built between Fairbanks and Valdez. Who today remembers Sloss?

A decade later the Alaska Railroad was pushing its way north from Seward. At Turnagain Arm construction crews built a tent city they alternately called Ship Creek or Woodrow. Streets were laid out in a grid and given starkly utilitarian names using only numbers and letters (e.g., 4th and G). Today, of course, we know this town as Anchorage.

Point Manning on the Arctic coast got its name in 1826 when famed explorer John Franklin thought he was looking at the mainland. Geographers later realized the point is actually surrounded by water, and today it's known as Barter Island.

The list goes on: Barrow got its name because it was easier for white people to say than Utkiakvik. So too the Sag River on the North Slope (short for Sagavanirktok). Eek, a small village on the Kuskokwim delta, is the rare example of a Native name that was actually lengthened, not abbreviated—it was originally spelled Ik.

What these examples demonstrate is that names are much more than just words. A place name is the product of the sociopolitical context in which it is bestowed. When that context shifts the name might not be as appropriate as it once seemed. To wit: Naming the main drag in downtown Fairbanks for Francis Cushman was a slam dunk in 1903—city leaders hoped to earn the patronage of the congressman from Washington state—but today nobody has the slightest idea who he was.

The People's Republic of Ester, as readers of this publication well know, has its own history of multiple names. That story has been told many times before, but a recap for the unfamiliar: The separate but adjacent towns of Berry and Ester underwent a merging of sorts in 1910 when the post office of the former moved to the latter but kept its original name. Not until 1965 did the Berry Post Office officially become the Ester Post Office.

Despite this confusion of names, it is the judgment of this writer that Esterites suffer no discernable identity crisis. Whether cynical or disillusioned may be attributed to other causes.

HOIST
a
GLASS!

◆◆◆◆◆

The final two chapters of this book were first published in the
Anchorage Daily News *and are included here as a bonus for*
those readers both interested in Alaska history and who have
made it this far without quitting the book. Both appeared as
"anniversary columns"—the first in April 2008 on the seventy-
fifth anniversary of the repeal of Prohibition in Alaska, and
the second in July 2008 on the fiftieth anniversary of President
Dwight Eisenhower signing the Alaska Statehood Act.

BEER DRINKERS IN Alaska require no particular reason to enjoy a frosty
mug, but they may nonetheless wish to raise a glass and toast the repeal
of the Bone Dry Law. Prohibition in Alaska ended April 11, 1933, making
legal, for the first time in fifteen years, the sale and consumption of
alcohol.

About two decades earlier, the temperance movement had reached
Alaska and was gaining momentum. In 1915, Territorial Governor John
Strong noted the rising tide of support for prohibition and believed a vote
of the people was necessary to decide the issue. James Wickersham,
Alaska's territorial delegate to Congress, ascribed the sentiment to dis-
content with the unruly, unkempt saloons that he called a disgrace to
every community where they operated.

Barrels of beer being offloaded at Nome on June 16, 1908. O.D. GOETZE, GOETZE
COLLECTION, ANCHORAGE MUSEUM, B01.41.185

The increasing political clout of women also proved a decisive factor
in the prohibition cause. Alaska had granted women the right to vote in
1913 (a full seven years before the U.S. followed suit with the 19th Amendment) and Strong believed a territory-wide referendum banning alcohol
would pass easily with this new voting bloc squarely behind it.

The territorial legislature put such a vote—"as to whether or not
intoxicating liquors shall be manufactured or sold in the Territory"—
before Alaskans in 1916. It passed by a more than two-to-one margin.
The Alaska Bone Dry Law took effect on January 1, 1918. Two years later
the 18th Amendment banned alcohol throughout the country.

In the ensuing decade prohibition proved a failed experiment. Originally proposed as a solution to all manner of social problems tied to
liquor consumption, the act succeeded only in spawning a whole new

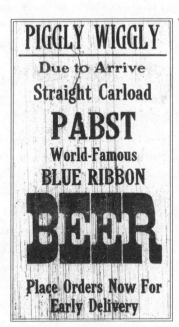

Piggly Wiggly newspaper advertisement on April 8, 1933, three days before the official end of Prohibition in Alaska, announcing the imminent arrival of beer in Fairbanks. FAIRBANKS DAILY NEWS-MINER, 4/8/1933, PAGE 4

realm of criminal activity—bootlegging, moonshining, and the attendant fraud and corruption in the illicit trade.

By 1933, the experiment was over. The 21st Amendment repealed the 18th, and states and territories were left to regulate their own liquor laws. One after another brought back booze. (Alaskans may be either proud or ashamed, depending on your point of view, to know we were the second to end prohibition, just a day after Michigan became the first.)

Alaska officially repealed the Bone Dry Law on April 6, 1933. It is worth noting the act ended prohibition in Alaska for whites only. Strict anti-alcohol measures for Alaska Natives, first put in place in 1867, remained in effect until 1953.

On April 11, the territorial legislature enacted laws governing the manufacture and sale of alcohol, as well as licensing requirements for bars, restaurants, and hotels. That same day, Ketchikan mayor John H. Davies became the first Alaskan to drink a fully legal beer. His pint bottle, which sold for 25 cents, was part of the first shipment of ten cases shipped via barge from Seattle.

A week earlier, in anticipation of the big day, the Piggly Wiggly in Fairbanks took out an ad in the local newspaper that announced, "Due to Arrive—Straight Carload—Pabst Blue Ribbon BEER—Place Orders Now For Early Delivery." Sadly for Fairbanksans, the shipment slated for delivery on April 17 didn't actually arrive until a week later. In Seattle, as throughout the country, demand was far outpacing supply.

The poor folks in Nome, however, faced a wait of at least two months. Only with the arrival of summer and thawing of the frozen Bering Sea would barges be able to reach the town. And in the interim? No problem, reported the *Nome Nugget*. Locals could simply rely on supplies of their "famous homebrew" (a tactic no doubt employed for the fifteen years prior). "We expect," the *Nugget* wrote, "the first steamers will be loaded to capacity because Alaskan frontier people like their beer, or what have you, on the hip."

Eight decades later and the statement still rings true.

TWO HISTORIC
DAYS
for
ALASKA—
ONE PRIVATE,
ONE PUBLIC

◆◆◆◆◆

It is a commentary on the complexities of the United States Congress and the Office of the President that the fate of any particular piece of legislation often rests on factors completely unrelated to the bill itself. The Alaska Statehood Act was no exception. Some senators, especially the Southern Democrats, opposed Alaska statehood on the grounds that her Congressional delegation might support civil rights legislation. President Eisenhower, too, was not immune from such extraneous considerations, as this column describes.

When President Dwight D. Eisenhower signed the Alaska statehood bill on July 7, 1958, he did so privately in the White House without inviting any of the Alaskans who had worked so tirelessly on the cause for more than a decade. In the presence of a single aide, as well as a few photographers and reporters hurriedly summoned for the event, Eisenhower affixed his signature, handed the bill off, and said, "Okay, now that's forty-nine."

He neither looked up nor smiled as the flashbulbs began popping. He flashed his trademark grin just once as he departed the room.

Eisenhower had long been lukewarm on statehood for Alaska. The former general recognized the strategic global position of the territory and, with the Cold War in full swing, was reluctant to cede any federal

President Eisenhower at his desk signing the Alaska Statehood Act on July 7, 1958. AP/WIDE WORLD PHOTOS/CHARLES GORRY

Eisenhower signing the proclamation admitting Alaska as the 49th state on January 3, 1959. ERNEST GRUENING PAPERS, UAF-1976-21-289, ALASKA AND POLAR REGIONS, RASMUSON LIBRARY, UNIVERSITY OF ALASKA FAIRBANKS

lands so vital to the national defense. A proposal to divide Alaska in half—statehood for the more populous southern regions, and all lands to the north and west set aside as a military reserve—even proved palatable to some residents if it was the only way to bring Eisenhower onboard.

From a political standpoint, the Republican president further resisted statehood knowing Alaska would likely send an all-Democrat delegation to Congress. This was one of the primary objections in the Senate and something that did indeed come to pass.

Eisenhower firmly supported statehood for Hawaii, however, endorsing the cause in three consecutive State of the Union addresses (1953–55). In January 1958, the president finally voiced support for Alaska statehood, but only if Congress considered a Hawaii bill simultaneously. Immediately after signing the Alaska bill, Eisenhower issued a statement again calling on Congress to admit one more. "I personally believe," he stated, "that Hawaii is qualified for statehood equally with Alaska."

Many in Washington speculated that Eisenhower, in signing the bill in private, simply didn't want to be photographed with a bunch of congressional Democrats who comprised the majority of statehood backers. Whatever the case, his action in no way incurred the wrath of Alaskans. They were plainly overjoyed and too busy celebrating to be offended.

The next ceremony was very much public.

On January 3, 1959, Eisenhower signed the official statehood proclamation in the presence of a number of Alaska dignitaries: Senators-elect Bob Bartlett and Ernest Gruening, Representative-elect Ralph Rivers, former territorial governor Mike Stepovich, acting governor Waino Hendrickson, and Bob Atwood, publisher of the *Anchorage Daily Times*. Also present for the occasion were Vice President Richard Nixon, House Speaker Sam Rayburn, and Interior Secretary Fred Seaton.

Following the signing, Eisenhower handed out souvenir pens to the Alaskans. He caught himself with a nervous laugh while calling Stepovich "governor"—not only had Stepovich resigned the position some months before in order to run (unsuccessfully) for the U.S. Senate, but in signing the proclamation just moments before Eisenhower had done away with the post of territorial governor altogether.

A forty-nine star flag was then unfurled, featuring a symmetrical arrangement of seven rows of seven stars each. Eisenhower turned to Bartlett and good-naturedly made his aesthetic disagreement known. He preferred four rows of six stars alternated with five rows of five. "But I was overruled by all my advisors," Eisenhower explained with a chuckle. When Hawaii came along, the president continued, he was going to recommend five rows of six stars and four rows of five stars, the design ultimately chosen.

The president concluded the ceremony by pledging his cooperation to the three Democrats of the Alaska congressional delegation: "I hope we can all work together."

The men got that chance just two months later when Bartlett, Gruening, and Rivers all voted for the Hawaii statehood bill, which Eisenhower eagerly signed into law.

ACKNOWLEDGMENTS

First and foremost, I would like to thank Deirdre Helfferich, editor and publisher of *The Ester Republic*—not for printing my columns month after month, nor for publishing a unique periodical that provides news and views found nowhere else in Alaska, but for all she does to make Ester a better place for everyone to live, work, and play. The sheer volume of volunteerism she performs can hardly be measured. I am certain she doesn't get thanked enough, so, in an effort to correct the imbalance— thank you, Deirdre.

As a writer of a regular column on Alaska history, I am constantly trolling for interesting topics. Many originate in casual conversations with friends and colleagues, most of whom probably don't realize I am test-driving a future column on them while we speak. For helping me develop those ideas I am indebted to Rich Ackerman, Jo Antonson, Michael Carey, Libby Casey, Terrence Cole, Ed Davis, Russell deForest, Jack de Yonge, Jim Ducker, Mary Ehrlander, Richard Fineberg, Bill Fuller, John Haines, Mike Hawfield, Steve Haycox, Ron Inouye, David James, Frank Keim, Paul Krecji, Dave Lacey, Larry Landry, Sean McGuire, Katie Oliver, Terry Reilly, Katie Ringsmuth, Jonathan Rosenberg, Rich Seifert, Mike Walleri, and Alison York.

Special thanks to Bridget Burke, Rachel Meade, Lisa Morris, Rose Speranza, and Marge Thompson at the Alaska and Polar Regions Collections, Rasmuson Library, University of Alaska Fairbanks, for their invaluable research assistance. I also wish to acknowledge and thank Sue Sprinkle and her staff at 5th Avenue Design for doing a great job on the cover design and layout of the book.

For generously providing the photographs that illustrate this volume I thank Jon Buchholdt, Merritt Helfferich, Robin Hiebert, Galen Lott, Charles Mason, Bevinne Morse, Ed Plumb, Wada Jujiro Kensho-kai, Gail Goedde and Sandy Johnston at Alaska State Library, Linda Epstein and

Erik Hill at *Anchorage Daily News*, Julia DeVore at Anchorage Museum at Rasmuson Center, Matthew Lutts at Associated Press, Danielle Kaltz at *Detroit News*, Kathy Struss at Dwight D. Eisenhower Presidential Library and Museum, Debra Hershkowitz and Cornelia Schnall at Landov Media, Keith Showalter in the State of Alaska's Office of the Governor, Lynne Snifka and the student journalists at *The Sun Star*, Megan Friedel and Mariecris Gatlabayan at University of Alaska Anchorage, Ned Rozell and Chisato Jimura at the UAF Geophysical Institute, and Christina Burtner and Nancy Hines at University of Washington.